Amazon   £5-07

D0308217

Copyright 2011 by Lorca Damon

Autism By Hand

by Lorca Damon

Introduction

I never wanted to write this book. I can't write this book, it hurts too much. But I have to because this book wasn't there when I needed it. It's not a human-interest story or a self-help book or an instruction manual on how to raise an autistic child. It's simply a well-thought out laundry list of everything I did to help my daughter be the best person she could become and I did it in the dark because this book wasn't there for me.

My daughter, Carrie, was diagnosed almost seven years ago. With everything. PDD-NOS, Autism Spectrum Disorder, Static Encephalopathy, Bipolar Disorder, and in the words of one specialist, Full-Blown Autism. I didn't even know that last one was a real medical condition.

Fortunately, Carrie was very young when she was diagnosed. She was barely thirteen months old when her pediatrician first mentioned that he was concerned about the fact that she wasn't reaching her milestones. The fact that she wasn't able to walk, talk, drink from a cup, or sit up without help should have worried me, too, but she was my smiling, pudgy little baby and I wasn't very concerned.

It wasn't until a different doctor voiced his concerns that I really began to wonder. This doctor told us Carrie's situation was, quote, "very bad." He wrote out a lengthy list of things we needed to do: EKG, CT scan, Early Intervention, Speech Assessment, Physical and Occupational Therapy Assessments, and more. I would love to say that all of this happened very quickly, but time and paperwork move at a snail's pace, especially when you're an anxious mother left with ominous news that there could be something wrong with your child and you're relying on tax-supported agencies to step up to the plate. Over the next several months we saw professional after specialist after expert until finally we were given a final diagnosis: Carrie was somewhere on the autism spectrum and none of the specialists we saw seemed to think she was anywhere close to the high-functioning end of the arc.

Like most parents in my situation, I dove in head first in trying to find out everything I could about autism and how it was going to affect my child. Unfortunately, more often than not the books I could find were only about theories on autism or current research or how bad the future could be for my child or the different ways that autism affects boys. None of that was helpful or reassuring. I didn't need to know the scientific history of autism, I needed to know how to potty train my daughter. I needed to know how to teach her to talk or what to do when the day finally came that she had to go to school or had a crush on a boy or got her period. Was she ever going to have a job, a checking account, and a car payment? All the research that was being done to make discoveries down the road didn't help me with my daughter's struggles today.

This book doesn't contain any medical information or scientifically-proven research because I am not a doctor or a researcher. And God bless those people who are sweating it out in laboratories and working themselves to death day-after-20-hour-workday to learn all they can for autistic people. I am, however, a teacher and a mother who has been there, so this book is simply the strategies that I learned from working with my autistic child. Basically, it's the book I prayed for but never found when I was trying to reach through the cloud that surrounded my daughter in order to pull her out into my world. Some of it might help other children, but not all of it will fit all kids with autism. Of course, some of it might even help some of the struggles that parents with "normal" children face.

I feel compelled to warn you that this book is not politically correct and does not spare your feelings. I'm basically telling you like it is the way your best friend would if she wasn't worried about hurting you and if she didn't feel like she doesn't have the right, just because she doesn't have an autistic child. You're going to hate me sometimes while reading this, other times you might feel like you should call the authorities and have my poor baby taken from what must be a child-rearing torture chamber. In the end, I really hope it was nothing more than the information you needed to hear, even if you wish I'd told you all of this a little more lovingly. Time's a wasting, there's not enough time to care about not stepping on your toes. Every day that goes by is another day that your child slips a little farther away. So read on and do all that you can for your family and your child.

Chapter 1: Get Over It

It's time for tough love: your child is autistic. Stop saying he's "a little bit autistic," or my favorite, "he's somewhere on the spectrum." Guess what? We're all somewhere on the spectrum! We're at the "not autistic" end! And please stop referring to your other children or your autistic child's classmates with cute little labels like "neuro-typical." They're normal. Your autistic child is not. I didn't say that was bad and I'm not suggesting that you can call your kid names or introduce him as Rain Man, but it is a statistical fact that most of the kids in the world are not like your autistic child, so by the freaking definition of the word, your child is not normal. There, I said it. Now we can move on.

And that's great advice for any family with any child who has any difference about them. Accept it and move on. I would rip off my own arm and eat it raw if it would make my child normal, but the sad fact is it won't. So why waste time and tears over the child I thought she was going to be instead of marveling at the beautiful creature she already is? It used to hurt a great deal that she isn't going to have the future I planned for her every time I rubbed the rambunctious bump in my pregnant tummy, but I had the funeral for that dream and have moved on. The pain gets less and less every single time she smiles at me or tells me she loves me.

Here is a great exercise. Your first assignment is to find somewhere alone, whether it's your backyard or your closet, maybe your garage. Go there right now. I want you to raise your arms high over your head and scream, "WHY?" as loudly as you can, over and over until you're hoarse. Then I want you to wait for the answer.

Guess what? You're not getting one. And even if by some miracle God sent the little naked cherubs down with a banner that explained it all, that told you every single thought process behind why you have to have a child with special needs, it is not going to change a thing. You have my permission to waste your life and your happiness crying out for answers, because that means there will just be more room on the happy bus for the rest of us. You officially hate me now, don't you?

Let's pretend that next week scientists will announce that they have unlocked the secret as to the causes of autism. Maybe you smoked pot in college, or you live in a house drowning in lead paint, or your zodiac sign was in the wrong house when you got pregnant. It's not going to change a thing, so get past it already and get to work on equipping your child to live in a world that doesn't meet his needs.

Chapter 2: Toolbox

When we received the first inklings that something was wrong with Carrie, it actually took several months to even hear any kind of diagnosis. We began with the easy things, like hearing impairment or determining if there were any developmental issues in the brain. Since autism is so subjective to some professionals, we even had doctors who told us it wasn't possible to diagnose her at such a young age or even that there was nothing wrong with her.

I remember waking up one morning in a fog and feeling this compulsion to drive to the local retail store. I placed a massive plastic bin in my cart then I went aisle by aisle, throwing in random things that could be used in any way. Toys, games, household objects, even a couple of things that I found in the automotive section. Whether or not Carrie was autistic was yet to be determined, but she was obviously delayed and every day that I wasted would be one more day that she would have to catch up later.

We kept that plastic bin in the living room and used it constantly. Everything was on hand for any moment of the day that we could do something with Carrie. I think I still even have the bin somewhere, probably stashed in the shed holding scuba fins or something, because Carries has aged up into more technological tools and toys. But I still can't bring myself to throw away that bin because it was so important in the beginng.

Here are the things that I kept on hand for working with Carrie. Some of these might be godsends for you, some of them might be the stupidest thing you'll ever try. Nothing here costs more than $20 so try it if you think your child will respond. I'd love to sell this as a whole kit, maybe with my own infomercial on Saturday morning television, but I'm just too lazy.

Mirrored wrap-around sunglasses, the bigger and cheaper the better. You might want to get a few pairs of these glasses because some of them are bound to get broken in all the play and unfortunately, in the occasional tantrums, both your tantrums and your child's. The point of the glasses is actually very simple. When you put them on they look kind of weird, which attracts your child's attention, but when he looks at your glasses he will see himself, which is kind of intriguing. More importantly, the glasses are blocking out a large portion of the overwhelming information that is provided by the human face.

Think of it this way: your eyes tell so much about your mood, but they also contain eyelashes that flutter, eyebrows which might have one or two hairs standing up in a distracting way, and if you're the mom (or hey, I guess if you're that kind of dad, who am I to judge?) you might be wearing colorful or smoky eye shadow and eye liner. Around your eyes there might be crazy little creases that the rest of society calls crow's feet—sorry, truth hurts, I have them, too—but those lines are weird to an autistic child. They are also the source of so much information about your mood, whether you're making happy eyes at your smiling child or whether your eyes have turned a glowing red because you're about to strangle the little dear. Basically, your eyes are so overwhelmingly distracting that looking at them is nearly impossible. When my glasses were not handy, I have even just planted myself in front of my daughter and talked to her with my eyes closed, just so she wouldn't be so overpowered by the intensity that is the human eye.

Several pairs of white gloves (winter kind, hardware store kind, jazz hands kind, doesn't matter, so long as they're white so you can write on them and light-weight enough that you won't feel stupid wearing them everywhere you go for the rest of your life. I'm kidding. No, I'm not.) The title of this book came from the use of my hand as a visual teaching aid to my daughter. Everything from how long it was until her birthday to how many bites of peas she had to eat came to her from looking at my hands, not my eyes. I would show her with my fingers how many words she had to speak. When she was screaming she could watch a countdown on my fingers of how much longer she could scream. The days of the week and months of the year were written in bright colors on the fingers so I could help her understand everything from what time we were going swimming to when Grandma was coming to visit. The gloves will be the calendar, the clock, the countdown timer, and more. So stock up. Before I thought to use gloves, all of this was written on my fingers in Sharpie. After I finally thought to use gloves so I would look less stupid with a hand-drawn Technicolor tattoo on both hands, I literally kept all my gloves clipped to my belt loop with a carabineer hook so they would be handy a million times a day.

Yoga ball. A lot of autistic kids DESPISE being off balance due to their weakened proprioception and vestibular senses. So slap him up on that ball and bounce him 'til his fears go away. I'm just kidding. Sort of. The yoga ball will be vitally useful when it comes to physical therapy, occupational therapy games like catching and throwing, and processing verbal commands like, "Roll the ball to me! Now roll it to Daddy! Now roll it to the couch!" You might even find that your child likes the feeling of bouncing or belly-rolling on it, to the point that he will take out the yoga ball and work out some of his energy on his own.

El cheapo plastic cups in rainbow colors, but all alike, and with maybe five of each color. I don't mean the disposable kind, but if you go to where they sell kids' dishes in any discount store you should find stacks of sturdy plastic plates, cups, and bowls in different colors. Buy several cups of each color. We stacked them, we kicked them with our right foot and then our left foot, we placed small objects carefully in each one, we lay on our backs on the floor and balanced them on our noses, we walked with them on our heads. They are absolutely limitless and the best part is they can go in the dishwasher whenever you've played with them a little too much.

Wooden puzzles of everything under the sun. Enough said. Wooden puzzles hold up better than cardboard and the pieces make a really satisfying clacking sound when you play with them. Plus, we had ones with large, chunky knobs for handles on each piece, bought from Sam's Club. They were more expensive than cardboard, but these puzzles had to hold up for years of play.

Stacking blocks, preferably the old fashioned wooden kind. Same story as above. They make a great noise, they're very durable, and they're generally inexpensive. Again, they can be stacked, they can be counted, the colors and numbers on the sides can be counted and named, the possibilities are endless.

Beads and plastic lacing string. Thread the beads onto the string for fine motor skills, count them to reinforce mathematical logic, sort them by color and make patterns with them, whatever. One of the greatest things you can do with them is have them handy and NOT let your child put them in her mouth. Inappropriate mouthing is a big problem for many autistic kids so this temptation will help them learn that it is unacceptable.

A stuffed animal (this one's tricky…once you know which one your child prefers, you have to immediately run back to the store and buy up all of that one in case something happens to it)

Your child might struggle for the rest of his life with making friends. You will literally have to teach him how to play with other people, how to take turns, how to have a conversation in line in the grocery store. The animal is far less threatening than a person, so he can be the guinea pig. Unless he's actually a guinea pig, then you can pretend he's something else.

Stompers. Buy these or make them, but they're the things that we played with in elementary school PE that we had to hold the strings and walk on. Again, your child may absolutely loathe and detest being off balance and perched on some stompers. So keep doing it. Practice stomp cry, practice stomp cry, repeat. One day he will laugh while he's stomping.

Filmy scarves . The best thing about scarves or squares of fabric with that light-weight, see-through quality, is that they don't move very fast. Did you know that beginner jugglers will often start out with scarves, since it allows for time to throw and catch? You can teach your child to make the TH sound by saying it through a scarf and trying to make it move, you can teach him to blow bubbles in the pool or blow his own nose by using a scarf. He can catch it when you throw it in the air because it's moving in slow motion, he can cover his head with it to learn how to be silly.

Bubble liquid and every known contraption for making bubbles. Well, duh, they're bubbles. They're awesome. And they're surprising. How many objects do you hold throughout the day that suddenly disappear? And I don't mean chocolate. I know where that went.

One great thing about bubbles is the facial motion required to actually make the bubble is important in feeding and speaking. Exercise those muscles by sitting outside and making a mess. Speaking of making a mess, use the bubbles to help your child overcome sensitivity to certain textures, in this case, slimy, by getting bubble liquid everywhere.

Play Doh and every known contraption for molding Play Doh. Well, duh, it's Play Doh, it's awesome. Kidding. However, if you follow the GFCF diet that is mentioned later in this book, be very careful with Play Doh. It's made from wheat flour and some autistic kids will eat it to get their fix of gluten. I finally had to start making my own Play Doh out of rice flour because Carrie ate it constantly.

Any toy you can get your hands on that does X when you do Y. For example, Carrie had a tower that made noise when you dropped the special blocks down the chute. We wore it out and had to buy another one, because she finally learned that X happens when you do Y. The rest of us figured that out the first time we tried it, but it took her a couple of years. She finally got there.

Flash Cards of every type Carrie had dozens of little boxes of flash cards, just cheap ones available from the retail store.

We did picture words, letters, animals, numbers, we even had a set of Flags of the World and U.S. state flags. It wasn't about making her memorize flags, but about getting her to see the connection between an object in my hand and the name that it has. Think of the scene in The Miracle Worker where Helen Keller finally makes the connection between the water coming out of the pump and the crazy-stupid thing that weird lady kept doing to her hand! I actually kept the flash cards on a shelf in Carrie's closet for focused time.

Carrie wasn't fully potty trained for a long time (you'll hear all those gruesome details in another chapter) and I moved her changing table into her closet, mostly to make room for the toys that were getting bigger and bigger as she got older. But I realized she was still and calm while laying on the changing table, so every time we changed a diaper I would pull out a set of flash cards and go through a bunch of them before letting her down. That way it wasn't just hours on end of relentless and torturous study, but it was also a quiet time when both of us had the other's attention.

Once Carrie graduated to moving around the house on her own, I also used flash cards to make a word wall in our kitchen. When I ran out of pre-printed words that she knew, I made them on index cards. Every time she sat in her high chair we would run through some of the words. While waiting for the water to boil on the stove, I would scoop her up and let her touch the words as she said them. I even did it as a bribe: "Say three words and you can have a cookie." It's not like I wasn't going to let her have a cookie anyway, so what's wrong with reinforcing a valuable skill at the same time?

Here are some things you CANNOT have in your toolbox. Any toy or object that your child stacks repeatedly or lines up across your living room floor. We learned this one the really hard way. Carrie had these plastic McDonald's play foods, little palm-sized pieces of lettuce, tomato slices, molded French fries, shake cups, etc. Every morning she had to race out to the living room and spend about ten minutes getting them organized in a stacked arc across the floor. Then she could go play. She could LITERALLY hear if a piece fell over during the day, even if she was in another room. Then she had to race out to the living room to fix it. Every night I cleaned them all up before I went to bed, and every morning she RAN to the living room to check on them and put them back the way she had them. We didn't know this is bad. This is a crutch, a way of maintaining order in a confusing world. You would think you're doing her a favor, like we did, by bringing those toys everywhere so she could calm herself by lining them up. It's actually a stimming behavior and as a long as she had those toys, she didn't have to find other ways to cope with stress. We took them away so that she had to learn to cope.

This is a good time to mention the first horrible thing I'm going to say to you. You cannot let your child have his way, IF having his way means crawling further back into the box of autism.

I truly wish the rest of the world was going to crawl in that box with him, but they won't. The world is going to shut the door to his box and leave him in there, alone and in the dark. You MUST make him get out of the box and join you in the real world. If you allow your child to have unlimited access to some comfort item that allows him to keep daily life at arm's length, he's learning that he can retreat into the box. Once we realized that Carrie's play food was a tool she used to close out everything around her and retreat into autism, we had to take it away from her. I felt like a monster, but I wasn't. A monster would take them away for no reason.

One day, about a year and a half after we put them in the closet, I was cleaning things out and she saw them. She asked for them, and I thought to myself, "What's the harm? She's doing so great now!" She ran to the living room with the box and lined them up. They went back in the closet. I am happy to say that it's now about six years later and those plastic pieces are literally scattered like an I-Spy book across the floor of the playroom. She's learned to deal with the world a little better and no longer needs them. So be aware of things that your child fixates on, especially toys.

Chapter 3: Talking

Carrie hated to speak. To me, to herself, to the dog, to anyone. I swear to you this entire book happened because one day I snapped and it became a breakthrough. We were in the car and once again she barked a one-word demand at me: "Music." I had already been through a full day's worth of headaches at work and a sadly-smiling day care teacher who told me that Carrie had cried in the corner for most of the afternoon because another child had a birthday celebration in class and Carrie is afraid of the birthday song. Carrie demanded that I turn on the car stereo and I lost it. I held up my open hand where she could see it from her car seat and yelled, "You know how to speak! You will say five words to me or you will have nothing!" She was startled into silence for just a minute, then said, "I want music now please." The whole concept for everything I'm telling you was born because I refused to let her do her own thing. This is my world, and the rest of my world doesn't care if you're autistic.

When Carrie first began working with a Speech Therapist in Early Intervention, the therapist introduced sign language. It's apparently a very typical tool that therapists use, because I soon realized all of Carrie's therapists would reinforce the sign language that the speech therapist was teaching her. I signed up for classes at the university up the road, bought sign language books and DVDs, tried to teach my husband some of the basic signs so he would know if Carrie was trying to express her needs. You name it, I did it.

Carrie hated sign language. She hated to be touched and the best way to teach a child sign language is to hold their hands and help them make the signs, while praising their efforts. The second I reached out to grab Carrie's little hands, she was done with me.

The real paradox was every time she finally got over the emotional or social hurdle that was keeping her from interacting with me, just long enough to let me know she wanted something, I would grab her hands and make her sign for it. So she would leave. She finally noticed I wasn't functional furniture long enough to look at me and I drove her away by doing something over and over that quite possibly caused her a physical sensation of pain.

When I finally spoke to her Speech Therapist about it to let her know that we were not continuing the sign language effort at home, I think she was very disappointed in me. I think her disappointment stemmed from the fact the sign language has been extremely helpful to a lot of kids and families. It just didn't work for Carrie.

Once I had convinced myself that Carrie wasn't interested, I was able to justify that thought by realizing that teaching Carrie sign language was going to take a lot of time and study. I happen to be fluently bilingual, so I know what kind of effort goes into learning an entirely new language. If I was going to put that kind of effort into teaching Carrie to communicate, I'd much rather teach her to speak!

I do not mean to sound like I'm condemning parents whose children are not verbal. There are many autistic kids who have found that sign language or communication boards, even picture cards, are the only window they can successfully and happily use to communicate. Other specialists and educators wanted Carrie to try the little laminated pictures so she could just point to what she wanted. That just wasn't enough for me, but more importantly, it wasn't enough for Carrie.

This all goes back to my earlier explanation that the world isn't set up for your child to succeed just yet. If you adopt the attitude that your child can't do any better than THIS, then that's exactly what will happen.

I do not pretend for a minute that Carrie is going to grow up to be a NASA physicist. Am I a bad mother for thinking that she won't be? Of course not. I'm being realistic. But at the same time, if I don't do all I can to make her engage in the behaviors that the rest of the world uses, things like verbal and written skills, I just made the decision once and for all that she will never be a NASA physicist. Heck, if she won't speak because I didn't do all I could to make her, I just slammed the door on a lot of jobs. I made the decision for her that she will not enjoy life to the fullest. Even the kid at McDonald's has to be able to speak to say, "Do you want fries with that?" and look how badly our society denigrates that kid's occupation as some kind of metaphor for loser. He can talk, so he was already one step ahead of Carrie.

Here is how we were able to encourage Carrie to talk:

1. First, and this one sounds like a head-in-the-sand Captain Obvious thing to say, we required it. Once we knew that Carrie was physically capable of talking and that she had no hearing impairments, we were able to realize that what kept her from being more verbal was the aversion to the interaction with other people. To which we basically said, "Too bad." If you want a cookie, you're going to ask for it. If you want juice, ask for it. If you can't reach your toy, ask for it. Teaching this concept took try-after-tantrum-throwing-try and it's really tempting to make the screaming stop by just giving her what she wants. I'm sorry. I'm the mamma and what I say goes. Don't back down, this is too important.

2. I don't want to imply that there are NOT some children who are affected by autism to the degree that they cannot speak. My heart goes out to those families and children. But how did you discover that your child cannot speak? I have met some kids who can do nothing more than make various noises that indicate how they are feeling, so obviously I am not speaking about those children; picture

cards or assistive technology are perfect godsends for them. I do know several others who use nothing more than echolaelic speech, meaning they only repeat phrases they have learned somewhere. Without any research whatsoever, I would have to think about this from a common sense standpoint: if you can speak, you can speak. I know I'm making that sound incredibly simple, but it's not, it's far from simple.

3. If your child is able to repeat lines from his favorite movie, start to notice if he's using them appropriately. Is he screaming, "This is awesome!" when he gets to go inner-tubing for the first time? It's a line from SHARK BOY AND LAVA GIRL, and the main character says it when he gets to fly behind the two superhero kids. The autistic child I took inner-tubing screamed those exact words from that exact movie and was using that phrase appropriately, so can we at least believe that with focused effort we could get him to use different words to express excitement? You never know until you try.

4. As with all things involved in teaching anyone anything, you can't back down. If you let your autistic child believe that he has to speak to get juice at home but that he doesn't have to speak to get soda in a restaurant because it's just easier if you order for him, you have just told him that speaking really isn't all that important. If you need to hurry this up, have him hit your fists (feel free to leave the gloves

around before I replied, "Yes! She does! She has to try it!" That rotten little pipsqueak ate the entire bag, which I was happy to feed her bit by overwhelmingly sugary bit, simply because she tried it and decided she liked it. If she had never put it in her mouth, she would never have eaten it.

Don't get me wrong, this is not a story where I brag about force feeding my child a new food and getting her to like it. But I'm also not ashamed of myself. Had this story involved my normal child, yes, a social worker should probably have intervened, but where my autistic child is concerned, I had to do whatever it took to make her climb one more rung of the ladder out of the deep pit of autism. To this day I refuse to let her NOT try a new food, as long as I don't have any fear that it can cause an allergic reaction. She does not love broccoli, but she eats it. Ditto peas, carrots, eggplant, zucchini (that one even makes her cry occasionally, but she eats it), et al. Would you let your normal child refuse to eat any fruits or vegetables ever? If the answer is yes, don't tell me, because then I will judge you harshly for letting your child walk all over you. Let's just agree to disagree?

The steps for introducing a balanced diet:

1. Find the textures your child is comfortable with. Some kids adore anything with the consistency of mashed potatoes, others literally gag on it. Find what your child is happy with.

2. There is nothing wrong with using the "sneak" method of putting healthy foods in with the already accepted foods. Over time, you just slowly begin to do a sucky job at hiding the foods.

3. THE HAND: When you introduce a new food, with your glove show your child how many bites he has to eat. It is helpful to have far more bites of the food than you will require, say, ten leaves of spinach if you are only going to make him eat three. It feels less threatening to see a huge pile of this offensive crap then know that you only have to eat a miniscule portion. And please don't be weird enough to make some blanket mandate about how the kid has to eat twelve bites…I know adults who don't eat twelve bites of a vegetable in a given day, let alone one meal. Keep it small and manageable, giving your child the room to succeed.

4. Do not for even a second consider making your child eat a food that you are not willing to eat. If you refuse to eat Brussels sprouts on the grounds that you are an adult and you pay the bills around here, why are you wasting money and tears force feeding them to your children, autistic or otherwise?

5. Keep the foods simple. For a lot of autistic people, the problem comes in when the zucchini has been turned into a slimy, goopy casserole, or the broccoli is swimming in some kind of bright orange used-to-be-cheese sauce. Keep

the foods plain, either raw or steamed, without overwhelming seasonings.

6. Don't be stupid enough to back down. When you said three bites but you didn't successfully get your child to eat one complete bite before you let him leave, you just wrote something else on your hand: "I'm a sucker who doesn't have to be obeyed."

Chapter 5: Clothing

Many autistic children, Carrie included, would run naked 24/7 if they were allowed to do so. And I guess if it was socially acceptable, I would wear the same pair of jeans and the same comfortable white T-shirt every single day. The difference between an autistic person and me is that very term: socially acceptable. Whereas I understand that people will stop speaking to me if I wear the same clothes every day and I will probably lose my job when I start to smell, one of the hallmarks of autism is a lack of understanding for what is socially acceptable. That's why you have to step in and stop your child from being the walking poster child for all that is socially wrong. First, by making him wear clothes.

I was at a support group get-together once and one family in particular had a twelve-year-old son who could not stand clothes. The moment he exited their vehicle at our cookout, he stripped naked right where he was standing. And his parents said nothing, suddenly too engrossed in the chips and dip to notice that their junior high school-aged child was letting it all hang it out in front of a lot of people.

Maybe it's because we were supposed to be people who "understood," or people who knew what they were going through. In reality, what they were going through was a complete lack of respect, for their son's privacy or for the people around them. My two small daughters were treated to a peep show of a half-way physically grown young man, and this young man was now on display because, "he just hates to wear clothes." If this were not a situation where autism was involved, if a normal child was actually stripped of his clothes and left standing naked in front of gawking strangers, the parents would be in jail. Why is this young man's dignity any less relevant just because he's the one who took the clothes off?

He removed all of his clothes, as he proceeded to do every time I saw this young man, because the clothes his parents chose for him were a sensory hell. Instead of letting him choose his own clothes, or at the very least forcing the clothes back on him every time he took them off, they were basically saying to his face, "This is all you are capable of."

Unfortunately, every time someone who is unschooled in autism comes in contact with a naked preteen, that person will think of that naked child every single time she comes across any person with autism. When people meet my daughter and hear about her diagnosis, their minds will return to the time they witnessed a random autistic child shoving handfuls of food into his mouth in the food court in the mall because the mother was too busy or too weary to stop him, or the child smashing his forehead on the pavement and screaming while the parent stood by doing nothing. These people will judge all autistic people, my daughter included, on the way you allow your autistic child to behave. I would like to ask you not to do that to my child.

I once put the same pair of shoes back on my daughter's feet twenty-seven times in the space of ten minutes. That is neither a lie nor an exaggeration. It became a battle of wills. I didn't beat her, or yell at her, or call her ugly names. I simply stopped everything I was doing, planted myself on the ground next to her, and put them back on her feet every time she took them off.

I know what you're thinking. You either think I have no life, or I have no ability to pick my battles. And yes, in the long run, having shoes on her feet is not a major life skill. But it was about to get her kicked out of a really great academic preschool play program that had agreed to take her on a trial basis. Everything else about her behaviors and her abilities was perfectly fine as far as this school was concerned, but this preschool could lose its license for letting kids run around barefoot, both for health department regulations and from the fire marshal. Those shoes meant the difference between academic-readiness or not, and therefore they suddenly became very worth my time.

Carrie never did learn to keep her shoes on all the time. She did, however, learn that there is a time and place for barefoot (or bare-assed, in the case of the young man from the cookout) and there is a different time for keeping the shoes on. Parents who are willing to watch their naked child sprint across a picnic ground without any clothes on while sighing and rolling their eyes, explaining, "He just won't wear clothes," are idiots who have given up. If that scenario pertains to your child, stay home, turn off your television and cell phone, and work on wearing clothes until he gets it so that all of you can go out and enjoy a cookout. It might take a few days, it might take a few years, it might take throwing away every stitch of clothing you've ever bought and buying sixteen identical navy blue T-shirts because that's the one your child likes. Make it a priority. The rest of us thank you.

How to put that shirt back on your child. Again. And again:

1. No matter what happens, or where you are when your child strips, stay calm. Do not give in to the impulse to "shame" your child into behaving. Do not let others use name calling or any other hurtful tactic such as belittling. Your child is not naked because he's a sexual pervert or because he's nasty, he's naked because his clothes might be sending sensory input to his brain that he is in physical pain. And because, face it, naked just feels great.

2. If you are at home when the stripping happens, you MUST resist the urge to think to yourself, "It doesn't matter, we're staying home today." It does matter, because your child is going to be violently confused when three hours from now at the funeral home it's suddenly not okay anymore.

3. THE HAND: If you're at home and your child enters the room without clothes, put the clothes back on him. Say to

him, "You have to wear clothes for ten minutes," showing him your fingers. Then set your timer. After ten minutes, if he has not moved on to a different activity and still wishes to take off the offending clothes, tell him that he may take them off BUT remind him that it is only okay to do so because you are at home and he will be IN HIS ROOM. If he wants to come out to eat or watch a movie, he has to wear his clothes. Show him your hands again and say, "In one hour when we go to the movies (choose something he LOVES to do when you're concentrating on this skill), we will have to wear clothes again."

4. This last statement will sound very paranoid, and it might be. If you have no other compulsion to teach your child to keep clothes on, please think of it this way. How will you know if your child has been sexually assaulted or violated if he or she does not understand that other people are not to see you without your clothes on? Children who cannot speak up are an easy victim, at least in the eyes of a potential predator. We have taught Carrie in a non-threatening way that NO ONE is to see or touch any part of her that gets covered by a swimsuit UNLESS MOMMY OR DADDY IS THERE (this is to prevent her from being uncooperative at a doctor's office or emergency room). I've noticed that the times Carrie comes dancing down the stairs without her clothes on (because we're staying home!) she is

always at least wearing her panties. That's still not good enough, we wear clothes unless we're staying in our rooms.

Chapter 6: Potty training

I am an absolute genius at potty training. I can toilet train anyone and anything. I have actually offered to come to people's houses and potty train their stubbornly non-pottying children. For ten thousand dollars. Ten grand is what it would take for me to potty train someone else's child. I said I could do it, I never said it was something I wanted to do.

Think of potty training logically from your child's point of view, and this goes for any child, autistic or not. For my ENTIRE life I have gone to the bathroom in these convenient little packages that you dutifully wrap up into poop grenades and cart away, never to be heard from again. Now, all of a sudden, you took me to the store, bought me a really amazing pretty plastic chair that is exactly my height, and you want me to do WHAT to it?!?

Basically, potty training my child involved taking a week off from work and not going anywhere for nine days if you count the weekends. It involved a lot of nudity (ignore the previous chapter for a little while), mostly from Carrie, but from me as well, especially when she peed on me while sitting in my lap. It involved a little bit of nudity from older sister Ann when I would send Carrie into the bathroom with her sister to figure out what goes on in there, and yes, letting Carrie stand there gawking as I used the facilities as well. It involved a complex system of rewards in which

Carrie would receive one Skittle for every minute she sat on the potty, ticking those minutes off with the demonstration of my gloved fingers. We went through fourteen movies and six bags of Skittles on the first day.

One of the keys to potty training Carrie was recognizing that this was a skill she would have to develop when she was ready, so I purposely waited until she was almost four years old to begin. I've heard horrifying tales of parents who spent months trying to toilet train, mostly because they started when they were tired of buying diapers instead of when their children were showing an interest in using the restroom. I never intended to spend enough money to send her to college on four years' worth of diapers, but that's what it took.

One of the other important keys to this success was keeping the potty chair in the living room so she would have no reason not to have it accessible. It's also the reason for the nudity (well, half nudity, she still had to wear a shirt because we wear clothes in this house!). I admit, there were even moments when I caught the urine after a good bit of it splattered on the floor, but once it was landing in the potty chair and she was firmly seated, I praised her just as well as if she had made the decision to sit there herself.

By Wednesday of our week off from life, we were ready to go to lunch at Carrie's favorite restaurant. While Carrie was not very verbal at that time, she was able to understand a great deal.

Telling any child, "We'll go to Burger Kind for French fries as soon as you go pee pee in the potty," goes a long way towards getting results. Once she had used the potty chair, we bundled up in thick panties and headed off to the restaurant. We used the "restaurant potty" as soon as we got there, just to show her how exciting the bathrooms in fast food restaurants can be. We ate our lunch accident-free, then headed directly home to avoid any mishaps. It was a successful venture out for Carrie, one that we talked about a lot together.

Here's how we enjoyed a modicum of success with potty training:

1. Starting a couple of months before you plan to start your full-fledged potty training, stop being in such a rush to change a diaper. Don't call the authorities on me, I'm not suggesting for a minute that you let your child wallow in his own excrement for hours on end. But the less time your child spends with his butt wet, the less urgency he'll feel for putting this diaper stuff behind him. All puns intended.

2. Once you begin potty training, arm yourself with your arsenal. Reward candies are important, along with LOTS of his favorite, especially forbidden, liquids. Soda, juice, kool aid, chocolate milk, you name it. The point is to make him have to use the bathroom a lot, not to build his nutritional standing in the community. It also helps to be able to say,

"You may have the soda as long as you are sitting on the potty."

3. Ditto for fibrous foods. Please don't make me say why.

4. Begin the potty training when you have the time to devote to it so that there's no confusion about why today I had to go in the potty but tomorrow I have to wear diapers to day care. Also, choose a warm time of year so that your child is comfortable without a diaper on.

5. Using your glove, show your timer fingers for how long your child has to sit there, or even better, for how long until your child can have another piece of candy. We had to use Skittles because using anything bigger was going to completely blow her blood sugar out of the water.

6. Be completely patient. I have a bad feeling terrible things are going to happen to your gloves during this escapade. At some point I know you're going to reach out and accidentally use your gloved hand to staunch the fleeting flow. It's okay, get another one. Better yet, keep lots of towels and carpet cleaner on hand.

7. Praise every success and do not be disappointed. All of those people whose children I offered to potty train were the parents of supposedly normal, non-pottying kids. One family had already been informed that their son would not be allowed to start KINDERGARTEN in a few months because he still wouldn't poop in the potty, instead insisting

that his mother put a diaper on him whenever he needed to poop. And this kid is supposedly gifted.

8. Do the world a favor. Don't be cute when you teach your child how to let the rest of society know he has to go. I have a supposedly totally normal friend who quietly whispers, "I have to puff," when she needs to use the restroom. I also have a medically-employed friend who "has to void." Don't teach your child something irritatingly darling and dainty. "I have to go to the bathroom," or, "I have to potty," are simple and to the point and are not too embarrassing, although with boys "bathroom" sounds more manly than "potty." More importantly, those phrases are universally understood by any adults who will work with your child. It would be horrible if your child told his substitute teacher sixteen times that he had to puff before finally wetting his pants in his fourth grade classroom.

Chapter 7: Routine

We were supremely lucky to find out about Carrie's diagnosis at such an early age and I have to fully admit that not every parent is so lucky. At her young age she was already displaying the ominous signs of "something wrong," so she was already in Early Intervention under the catch-all label of Developmental Delay before the official diagnosis came along.

As an educator, I had some very rudimentary experience with autism, but one of the things I remembered was that they usually have a desperate need for routine. And who among us does not find comfort in knowing that when the alarm goes off, I get ready for work, have one cup of coffee, pack the lunchboxes, have a second cup of coffee, get the kids ready for school, fill a travel mug with coffee, then head off to drop them at school and go on to work? (Yeah, that was three cups of coffee before eight in the morning…don't judge me.) If anything goes wrong in there, it can wreak havoc on the entire day. If the alarm clock doesn't go off or the car battery is dead or there's not enough coffee to make three cups, it can start a downward spiral that colors the rest of the day.

Guess what? The rest of the world won't cater to your child's need for routine. It can't. If every person in the world got her way all of the time, it would interfere with my ability to get my way all the time. That was a joke. The simple fact is your child will not be able to follow his routine without any interruptions from time to time, and teaching him that he can have his every chronological whim is setting him and the rest of the people who care about him up for failure. The loud, tantrum kind of failure.

For example, just last summer we got all ready to go to the pool, just like we do most days during summer vacation. I packed the cooler full of drinks and snacks, we put on the swimsuits, we even put on the sunscreen (helpful parenting tip: put on the sunscreen at home, BEFORE you head to the pool…your kids are more likely to hold still for it since they aren't staring at an inviting swimming pool and all of their friends, PLUS sunscreen needs about fifteen to twenty minutes to soak in before they get wet). We drove the short distance to the pool only to find that the filter system had broken. The entire pool was a giant vat of dark green pudding and professional pool technicians milled around the deck dumping various (possibly illegal) chemicals into the pool to try to kill the algae.

My daughter went ballistic, and I mean, without even waiting to see if I said those fateful words, "Oh, we can't go swimming today." Of course, any child would be supremely disappointed by that scenario, but a child with autism would feel it even more acutely. Besides having the routine interrupted, I had led her to believe that she was going swimming. She was already wearing her arm floaties, for cryin' out loud! Nothing says,

"You're going swimming," more than putting on a swimsuit, sunscreen, and arm floaties. And then it didn't happen.

If you succumb to the belief that you will be helping your autistic child by maintaining a strict routine, you are setting him up for disappointment, tantrums, and the embarrassment that comes from losing control of himself in public. (This might be a good time to bookmark the chapter on Embarrassing Your Child in Public).

Here is how we taught Carrie to be a little more flexible. Notice, I didn't say really flexible:

1. Mess with their heads. No, I mean, literally mess with their heads. Carrie wore a Mickey Mouse hat every day all day long for months when she was very little. At first I thought she just really loved the hat because we had bought it in Disney World. Then, when I realized that she couldn't get out of bed without putting it on, I realized it meant more to her than just nostalgia. Around that time I read a really interesting book that talked about proprioception, and I made the connection between the tight elastic chin strap on the hat and Carrie's feelings of safety. The hat let her know where her head was and it's quite possible that she felt weird when she wasn't wearing it. Once I figured that part out, I was able to wean her off the hat and onto a headband, and from there, to having her hair pulled tightly into a

ponytail (it looked a helluva lot less weird than wearing the Mickey Mouse hat to preschool every day). But I would purposely change up the ponytail every single day, complete with the hair bow that went with it. Some days all of her hair went up into a middle ponytail, sometimes it was down low on her neck, sometimes on the side, other days just the top of her hair was pulled back. She would cry, and I would just tell her, "This is how we're doing it today, we did it the other way yesterday." That might be a little tougher if you have boys, but you can buy his favorite pajamas in six different colors and swap it up every couple of days, instead of doing what I used to do, which was buy ten pairs of those exact jammies so she would always have her favorite ones.

2. You can do a lot with food routines. Yes, I eat my snack at basically the same time every day, too, but unlike some autistic children it doesn't have to be six long Cheetos and eight short ones every day. Today it's Cheetos, tomorrow it's Doritos, the next day it might not even be a member of the chip family.

3. Afternoon movie is another good one. Carrie wore out a VHS copy of Riverdance because she had to watch it every day after she ate her breakfast. Guess what? Damn thing broke. I had bought it from the PBS membership drive, so it's not like I could just pop down to the store and get another one. We were up the creek. Screaming was

involved, and Carrie cried, too. So yes, let your child have movie time every day, but purposely change it up so there's a different movie. This would be a great time to get him to hit your gloves (or even better, speak) to tell you which movie he wants from the two or three choices you give him. You could also say, "Great choice! We'll watch this other one tomorrow," so he a) takes comfort in knowing that you're not changing everything in his life (he'll still have movie time) but b) realizes we're not going to watch today's movie again tomorrow. Carrie has become extremely resilient when it comes to having her sister say, "Which movie should we watch?" Of course she has her favorites, but she's also able to compromise, which is a skill adults have to help ALL children develop.

Chapter 8: The Concept of Time

Of all the individual life skills I could have chosen to give an entire chapter to, you might be wondering why I chose this one. In Carrie's case, her lack of understanding about time has led to more dramatic meltdowns than any other skill. It started from a very, very early age. Even worse, it took me a long, long time to realize that her inability to understand the passing of time (and I mean, the understanding of SECONDS passing, let alone months) was the source of a lot of her fear.

We seriously used to find it kind of amusing that she would scream in her highchair if you put down the spoon. I don't want to make it sound like we used to invite people over and say, "Hey, y'all, watch this," then put the spoon down just to make her cry. No, it was while we were feeding her baby food. If you put down the spoon LITERALLY just long enough to pick up and open another jar, she would go ballistic. I mean, tears, snot, choking sounds, the works. She would get so upset that sometimes she couldn't even eat that next jar, but more often she would just force it down while making sobbing, hiccuping sounds. We used to joke that she acted like a child who had never eaten a full meal in her life. Of course, we didn't know then that she was autistic, so it just seemed really weird to us.

Down the road, with the diagnosis stamped firmly across her forehead, there were other times that we noticed a weird correlation with time. If you were standing in the kitchen and pointed to the cookie jar, and asked, "Would you like a cookie?" she would lose it. Hysteria. One day my mother-in-law HAPPENED to be climbing up our front steps when this situation occurred. She raced in and grabbed Carrie from my arms, certain that I had slapped her little face or something. "No, I just offered her a cookie! I swear!" I know that woman didn't believe me.

And who would believe that? The problem was you couldn't offer Carrie ANYTHING unless you were holding it in your hand because she struggled with both object permanence and time. She had absolutely zero understanding that it takes .25 seconds to walk to the jar and grab a cookie. Many children don't get the concept of, "It's an hour until your friend comes over," but Carrie had zero ability to piece together that things happen in order or that they are still going to happen even if it's not happening right now.

Through the years, I'd love to tell you we figured out how to help her with this on a permanent basis, but it is still a struggle for her. In fact, all I can safely say we've been able to accomplish is to help her tone down her reaction to the disappointment of something not happening right now. She STILL to this day perseverates, meaning you have to tell her fifty-three times in a row, "Yes, we go to Disney World on Thursday." "Yup, on

Thursday." "Sure thing, kiddo, we go on Thursday." "Today is Monday, then it's Tuesday, then it's Wednesday, then it's Disney World Thursday." "I swear to God, we're going on THURSDAY!"

This was probably the single biggest use of the gloves in our household. I could hold up my bare, gloveless hand and tell her to say five words, because that's a counting skill and she eventually mastered that. The gloves, though, had the days of the week, the months of the year, the words "morning" and "afternoon," you name it. That's why we owned so many gloves. I seriously have had to write the names of the days of the week on my hand because I mistakenly thought it looked less conspicuous than the gloves, and it would have if I were going to the prison for the day where everybody had tattoos.

To show your child when something will happen, think about how far off it is. Is it happening six months from now or three days from now? Then use the correct glove to demonstrate, starting with where you are today. "Today is Monday (thumb), tomorrow is Tuesday (forefinger), the next day is Wednesday (middle finger), we go to the movies on Thursday (ring finger)." The visual glove gives your child something concrete to pertain to rather than the abstract concept of time. And nope, he's not going to get it the first time. He won't even get it the fortieth time. It's also possible that the five hundredth time you tell him, he didn't get it then either but he stopped asking because he finally realized you're just going to tell him the same thing again and he's bored with you. Either way, he went off to play happily instead of slamming his head on the coffee table some more.

This tactic can work with hours in the day just as well, if your child can absorb that concept. For hours in the day, we found it wasn't as useful for Carrie as a plain digital kitchen timer. I can simply tell her, "It's too early for snack, we'll have a snack when the timer beeps." This one takes a lot of practice, but it's great that your child will be able to see the timer actually counting down. First of all, that's a math skill, second, it might be calming to watch the numbers go backwards, and third, it tells him that this isn't abstract, I can SEE the time getting closer. Eventually Carrie got to where I didn't even have to actually set a timer for her, she was just able to process the remark, "When the timer beeps," to mean that something would be happening soon but not right this minute.

This is a great time to tell you that I hope you don't think my child is just better at this than yours. Please don't be misled for even one second. All of the tactics in this book took a lot of time and effort. Carrie NEVER got something the first time and there were hundreds of meltdowns over the years until she was able to process that what I was telling her was the truth. The gloves, the timers, the potty training, whatever, it all took practice and diligence, but in the end they helped her tremendously.

Here's how we helped Carrie with the concept of time:

1. First, we decided this was one of those things that was worth teaching her because it would mean that her life would be a lot less stressful. Would you like to go through life not knowing when ANYTHING was going to happen to you?

2. At first we would purposely NOT tell her stuff because we didn't want the tantrum when we couldn't make her understand that it wasn't going to be right now. All that did was cripple her by making her think life was one giant game of jump-out-and-do-something-to-you. We had to teach her a way to learn that things happen LATER.

3. Eventually, after lots of practice with the time techniques, we were able to start small. "We will go to McDonald's in twenty-five minutes." From there, we could talk about bigger things. It is March as I write this, and Carrie knows we're going on a camping trip to Texas in July. It takes a lot of practice though.

4. Make sure you set up easy goals so your child won't have to be patient for very long, then when he's mastered that you can move the time further and further away.

Chapter 9: Books and Websites That Were Helpful

I had to search far and wide for websites, books, and blogs that spoke to me. And the fault is almost entirely mine and my flawed personality. I have never benefited from hearing people complain about how hard it is for them or how bad things are in their situation. I attended a grand total of ONE autism support group meeting and never went back after witnessing two hours of a "my child is more autistic than your child" pissing contest. Some parents there actually rolled their eyes and muttered, "Just wait," when I mentioned my daughter hadn't started school yet.

And that could be why I never really connected with a lot of the books I would flip through in the bookstores. Once I read about how dark the writer's world was, I was done with it. At the same time, I also have zero use for any books in which parents make the claim, "My autistic child is amazing and I couldn't imagine him being any other way." Bullshit on you. I would sell my body to the lowest bidder on the nearest street corner if it would make Carrie be normal, not just because my life would be easier but because her life would be far easier. But it isn't going to happen, so why waste my life being unhappy?

I actually came across one website whose mission was to change the spelling of autism to AWEtism, because apparently autism is awesome. Tell me, which part of autism is awesome? The screaming tantrums? The walking skeleton of a child who doesn't eat? The boy who slams his head against the wall for hours at a time because it's the only way he can feel anything?

I really hope I'm just reading that wrong, and that their intention is actually more about making normal people see that autistic people are still worthy, valuable humans and that they have God-given rights, which I fully agree with. I don't agree with autism being a freaking awesome part of my life, though.

So I've found the most useful information in the genre of autism books that are coming out now written by autistic people. Temple Grandin is an obvious source of great insight, although most of her published works are about her field of study, animal behavioral science. The woman is a true genius in her given field, and the rest of us have just been blessed that she agreed to step away from her work long enough to write about what it means to be an autistic person.

Two other memoirs provided me with some very valuable information for how I raise Carrie. One of them was kind of tongue-in-cheek, with some sad parts and some amusing parts, the other was so downright depressing I had to force myself to sit and finish it, and I'm a better mom because I did. *Songs from the Gorilla Nation* absolutely broke my heart, but that's where I learned about Carrie's struggle with proprioception because I happened to read it during Carrie's Mickey Mouse hat stage. *Look Me In The Eye* was a tremendously interesting read as well, and it taught me a lot about how Carrie might process sensory information. Both books had their ups and downs for the authors, just like life does to us all, but in the end I was able to see that these are two successful, mostly happy people, despite whatever handicaps and trials autism brought to the table for them.

I have two other books that are as close to being instruction manuals as I could find, and both were very helpful. *Ten Things Every Child With Autism Wishes You Knew* had tons of stuff that didn't pertain to Carrie in any way, but it had just as much stuff that did. What I took away from that was the knowledge that autistic kids are as unique as normal kids and that there's no blanket protocol for reaching them. The same author also wrote *1001 Great Ideas for Teaching and Raising Children with Autistic Spectrum Disorders*, which had less theoretical information and a lot more practical advice than any other book I'd found.

I'm going to talk about the young adult fiction book *Rules* by Cynthia Lord later on, but it's worth mentioning here. It was a true glimpse into what day-to-day life is actually like in a household struggling to keep its head above water and about how epically failed a family can be when they're not keeping a positive attitude and working together.

Thanks to the advent of easy-to-use blogging websites, there are really great blogs out there. Even better, you can sign up to receive email updates on the blogs you like and receive each new entry as an email, saving you the time and effort of going looking. There are blogs specifically for families with multiple autistic children, kids by age group (so you aren't wasting time reading about potty training when your autistic kid is fifteen!), just boys, just girls, big families, little families, single parent families with autistic kids, kids who are on the diet, kids who couldn't do the diet, EVERYTHING. One website in particular is nothing but a warehouse of autism information published by the people who are living it, and that is www.autisable.com. That is one site that is so full of information you're going to have to spend a weekend just sifting through to see what speaks to you, but I'm sure if it's an issue you're facing, it's on there somewhere!

The trouble I kept coming across when I was searching for autism resources was I quickly got fed up reading about all the great resources parents could try because they lived near a metro city, if not actually in one. I live in rural Alabama, we don't even have a Starbucks, I know for a fact we don't have an autism play therapy group. We don't have music therapy, horseback riding therapy, or auditory integration therapy and I know we don't have a health food store that sells organic produce and macrobiotic foods. That's not to say that I can't find any of those things within a two-hour drive of here, but how often do I drive two hours each way so my child can bang on a xylophone and I pay $100 for the privilege and then head off to buy her an $8 carton of yogurt? I'm not dogging those concepts, I'm just saying that reading blog posts about people getting to try all these neat new things wasn't helpful.

You will find that one of the best sources of information for your child's specific needs will be to write your own blog. I know, I know, you'd have to do it between midnight and four am when you're just lying there doing nothing, but consider it. For your blog posts, you're going to get people who comment, and their comments will often be helpful suggestions for what they did in your situation. It may also be the wealth of information that some other family out there is desperate for.

Here are some useful websites, but this is just scraping the very edge of the dust on top of the particles on the barrel:

1. www.gfcfdiet.com
2. www.FHautism.com
3. www.allergygrocer.com
4. www.autisable.com

Chapter 10: Focusing On The Future

You can plan out your children's futures all you want to, but at the end of the day there are no guarantees. Terrible things like car accidents or unplanned high school pregnancies happen and they derail the future to some degree. Other times, nothing earth-shattering happens, but the plans just didn't work out, say, you thought you wanted your child to go to medical school but her burning ambition is to be a hair stylist. And there's nothing wrong with being a hair stylist, it's just different than you planned. The same is true with my autistic child, so I don't waste a lot of energy planning the future more than common sense dictates.

I admit that one of my stick-my-head-in-the-sand weaknesses is refusing to think about the future. And honestly, I don't spend a lot time worrying about my own future, let alone Carrie's. I truly don't have the energy, since I'm doing all I can to make sure this week works out for all of us. Also, I do have the luxury of having a spouse who is awesome at financial planning and thinking of the future, so I full-disclosurely admit that he takes care of the future, I take care of the present.

One of the first things we did when we started down this autism road was to learn a lot about where these kids end up, and I don't just mean physically end up, but independence-wise as well. Sadly, the books we were reading at that time were somewhat outdated because autism wasn't a huge nationwide topic when Carrie was a baby. I was reading books that had been written in the 80s, and no, kids diagnosed in the 80s didn't have the same access to therapies and education that they have today. But it was still scary.

We've always had a college account for Ann, but we looked into a different kind of account for Carrie. The money is there for her to go to college or vocational school, if that's something her future abilities will allow, but it's also not going to be heavily tax-penalized if we end up needing that money for her future care in a long-term residential facility. Something else we did was update our life insurance from term to whole life, which will cost us more in the long run but that we see as an investment. Someone with two normal kids who go on to medical school will probably not feel a burning need to leave their kids a million dollars when they die, but someone with a special needs child might. You do have to take into account the fact that by the time I die, one million dollars will not be worth as much as it is today, so it may not be the most prudent investment; just make sure it's not your only investment.

We also made sure to buy a house that is going to appreciate well. Everything about the house was planned out, at least as well as it can be. Sure, the county could decide to put a landfill behind our house and its property value would dive bomb, but we made very conscious decisions about this property so that its value will increase and leaving it to our children will actually be a good thing.

But money isn't the only consideration when you're planning for an autistic child's future. One of the things that sometimes eats at me is the fact that Carrie only has one sibling. That means all of the care and attention for Carrie will fall solely to Ann when I can no longer take care of her. We have a few family cousins and other extended family members, but logically they will all have their own families when I'm gone. I've even tried to talk my husband into adopting more kids (we decided not to have more of our own since one has epilepsy and one has autism), just so Ann would have some backup! By the way, he reminded me that "future caregiver" is not really the best reason to open your home to a child in need, so for now adoption's on the back burner.

Something that has become a concentrated effort on my part in the last two years is taking a keen notice of things that Carrie shows a particular interest or ability in. She is an incredible little artist, but only with the computer. She hates to use a pen or pencil because the little hand grasp is difficult for her. But she can create these really amazing drawings using the computer. Right away your mind might jump to architect, since she's so computer savvy, but no, her special interest is in cartoons. She draws these really detailed crazy-looking monsters and animals, and one of her best homework assignments ever was the time she had to draw pictures to go with her vocabulary words. She did the whole thing on our computer and printed it out herself. In first grade. It was truly incredible.

So I'm already looking into graphic design for her. The really important thing for me to remember is that this could all change. She might lose all interest in computers by next year. I have to remain flexible and resist the urge to decide, "Okay, this is great, she's going to live at home and go to the college up the road then become a graphic artist and live with her sister and work from home with the help of an assistant." It may not work out that way. I will admit, it looks really good from here, but the future isn't set.

But there's nothing wrong with taking a good look at your child and REALISTICALLY preparing him AND you for some kind of future. I am very prepared for the fact that if Carrie wants to go to college and if she is capable, she may still need someone to sit with her just like she does in elementary school. And I'm prepared for the fact that I might have to be that person. The college isn't going to provide a paraprofessional like her public school does. Heck, her school might not provide one for high school, and that person still might have to be me! It would mean quitting my job and not retiring on the timetable that I've set for myself, and I accept that.

If Carrie is able to live on her own, which her doctor whom we love has very seriously told us probably won't happen, she will still need assistance with things like getting around and maintaining a checkbook and filing her taxes . Again, that will probably be me, but the checkbook doesn't go away the day I die. There are all kinds of contingency plans that have to be accounted for.

Here's where we stand on Carrie's future:

1. Repeat after me. "I do not control the future. I will not waste a ton of energy creating needless stress for my family by trying to manipulate the space time continuum."
2. Now repeat after me. "I am not a moron, so I will build the foundation for my child to have a future."
3. Repeat this part too. "Armageddon is not a good retirement plan, for me or for anyone else. I will give conscious thought to being prepared for any outcome regarding my autistic child."
4. On a serious note, there are future plans you have to make TODAY. Who takes your children if something happens to you and your spouse? Are they prepared for a special needs child, or are these the people you planned back before you knew you had an autistic child? Where is your will located? Does the sale of your house fall into the hands of someone who will be responsible with the money and put it aside in safe investments for your autistic child's future? Some of the best people to meet with at this stage will be the administrators at a long-term care facility. No, you don't

have to sign over your house to them right now, but they can get you started in the direction of how to make good and reasonable plans.

Chapter 11: Vaccines

Yup, I was going to have to face the music on this one sooner or later. Practically every parent of an autistic child that you will ever meet will want your opinion on the vaccines. If you're unfamiliar with this topic as it relates to autism, then you're in good company, because so are the doctors who first published the study back some twenty-five-odd years ago.

Apparently, a study was published in a prestigious medical journal that linked vaccines to autism, specifically, the preservatives used in the MMR vaccine and a few others. The preservative back then was made from a mercury-based derivative. And there was lots of anecdotal evidence in the study. For example, Japan had the lowest industrialized-world autism rates and they don't give a single vaccine until age two (let's ignore the idea that the Japanese just might eat more mercury than anyone else on the planet since they are an island nation whose diet is almost exclusively oceanic fish). Plus, looking at the more commonly understood idea of autism, which is children who are perfectly normal until they reach toddlerhood and then regress, many parents dutifully took their children to get vaccines and then basically felt like they came home with a completely different baby.

I have told you before, I am not a doctor. But logically, all of those autistic children were also normal and then they ate their first French fries. Or rode on a merry-go-round. Or visited their grandparents in Florida. So what caused the autism? Was it the trip to Florida?

I do not blame the medical community for this one, at least not entirely. I do not believe for a minute that some doctor in England thought to himself, "I know how we can ruin a lot of people's lives by getting their babies killed from completely preventable diseases! Let's convince them that shots are evil!" More likely, I think a completely desperate and befuddled medical community was trying to give parents hope and closure.

I will admit to you openly that my daughter's diagnosis came at such an early age and that ALL of her current success is due to the fact that her doctor made a mistake. Her pediatrician had obviously read the same journal articles and subscribed to the same school of thought about the vaccines as those researchers. When I went to the appointment to get her 12-month shots, he would not give them to her because she wasn't reaching her milestones. He was afraid of vaccinating her if there were already "issues." The fact that he was wrong about the shots is irrelevant; his "concern" led us to get on the ball with more testing and Early Intervention, and for that I say he saved her life.

Picture it this way: let's pretend the vaccine-theory had already been debunked and he gave her the shots. Would it have made her MORE autistic? Of course not. Would we have floated along blissfully unaware that there was a problem for another year or so? Probably. And she would not have gotten the focused, concentrated help she needed. We would have wasted an entire year of her life, and even typing those words right now has made my eyes fill with tears and my breath catch in my throat. The ONLY treatment for autism available right now is INTENSE therapy, which is why I've told you already I don't have time to play around with hurting your feelings. And neither do you.

Now, here is where I've had several loud, angry, profanity-ridden arguments with quite a few people, my own relatives included: I fully believe we are over vaccinating our children in this country. Stop, don't close the book. Don't stick the pins in my voodoo doll just yet.

I didn't say that we should all just take our chances with the measles, and yes, I wholeheartedly agree polio caused widespread death and devastation. I'm talking about the cocktail vaccines. Carrie weighed eighteen pounds at her one-year check-up and she was supposed to get FOUR pokes at that appointment; each syringe contained more than one vaccine. She weighed less than our Halloween pumpkin that year! I just can't believe it's a good idea to stick her with that much stuff IN ONE VISIT. I PERSONALLY believe (meaning my own opinion, nothing more) that we are attempting to save tears, time, and money by squeezing a lot of chemicals into a baby. I'm sure there are doctors burning me in effigy right now, but that's the decision I've made for my family based on having just as many doctors scare the crap out of me since this process began for my family.

Allow me the luxury of repeating myself. VACCINES HAVE NOT BEEN PROVEN TO CAUSE AUTISM. VACCINES ARE NOT EVIL. YOU'RE A MORON IF YOU REFUSE TO GET ANY VACCINES EVER. There, I said it. All I'm saying is be informed and make wise choices based on what is best for your children.

Here is where we stand on vaccines for Carrie (and Ann, too, for that matter):

1. We do vaccinate our children, but not in massive doses. There is a pharmacy in the large city near us that sells the Measles, the Mumps, and the Rubella vaccinations in individual syringes instead of as the MMR shot. You have to go there to get it because there is no preservative in it. There. Everybody's happy. My kid won't infect yours with measles and there was no risk from the preservative (by the way, the U.S. stopped using the mercury-derived preservative in vaccines back in 1999, before my children were born).

2. We do not let our girls get more than one shot per doctor visit. I will come back as many times as I need to and I realize the health insurance isn't going to pay for me to go back every three months, but that's a financial decision I have to make for my own peace of mind.

3. In order to slow down the schedule of how often you receive vaccines for your kids, you will need an exemption form for your child's school. In my state it's referred to as, "The Blue Slip," and it has a place for your doctor or your pastor to sign as to why you're exempt (medical or religious reasons). Yet again, I am NOT telling you to go get a medical or religious exemption and never vaccinate!

4. We are very cautious about the "new thing" to come along. We didn't race out and get the supposed "cervical cancer" shot for our girls because I just don't trust it; when you have to be misleading in your national advertising campaign, you just might be hiding something. We also don't get vaccines for things that are not life-threatening. Yes, it is possible to die of the flu, but thanks to good medical care it is not as likely as it used to be back during the 1918 outbreak that killed millions.

5. Stay informed and follow the advice of medical professionals whom you trust. We have been blessed to have doctors whose advice I would follow to the letter, but we also had a doctor who diagnosed Carrie with fetal alcohol syndrome on her paperwork because "your

insurance doesn't cover autism." I'm not in a hurry to take advice from a guy who put "Mama's a drunk" on the paperwork so he could commit insurance fraud. There are just as many idiot doctors out there are there are idiot teachers, idiot bankers, and idiot power pole repairmen. Being a doctor does not make him any more or less human.

6. Most importantly, there are some entirely preventable diseases out there that are raging as we speak. YOU MUST prevent measles, rubella, tetanus, and polio, just to name a few. Those are so stupidly preventable that (in my humble opinion!) there is no reason to contract one of those diseases in America, allowing for the fact that there are parts of the world where those diseases run amok. And that short list was by no means comprehensive! Find out by making informed decisions with your trusted doctor.

Chapter 12: Public Safety

As the mother of a child who has serious issues with elopement (determined wandering away), I may have to be a little more paranoid about this stuff than you do. Carrie was three the first time the police found her walking along the highway about half a mile from our house. She had seen something interesting and beelined toward it before any of the THREE adults who were supervising the kids knew what happened. Of course, she had been gone only a matter of minutes before we began frantically looking for her, but the longer we looked for her in the wrong places, the farther away she got.

I've heard many, many scary stories about kids who have gotten away from their families and there are tons of safety devices on the market that will help you. I think my biggest worry was always that Carrie would wake up during the night and get out of the house before I knew she was gone. We have a motion-detector at knee-height right outside our bedroom, so if Carrie walks past her room toward the stairs, it will go off. We also have the little magnet sensors on our doors and windows that beep pleasantly if any door or window opens. Those have proven to be sufficient for our home, although with more determined kids, there are even devices similar to a prisoner ankle bracelet, but we haven't needed to go that far.

One of the best things you can do is take the time to go to the police station and the 911 dispatch office to let them know about your child. For the police, ask if they can keep a file with your child's information and photograph in case of elopement. That way, they're not wasting time trying to get a picture of your child as your son gets farther and farther away. NOTE: this is an extreme thing to do and you don't want to appear to be a paranoid parent, so this probably isn't really necessary unless you know for a fact this is a real likelihood for your child. For the 911 dispatcher, though, they can keep the information in the computer to alert firemen or paramedics that an autistic child lives in the home. That way, if there's ever a fire, they know to look for a child who may or may not be able to respond to commands or give their location when the fireman asks, "Is there anyone in here?" Autistic kids (and kids in general) might hide from the firemen during a fire, so the dispatcher can alert them ahead of time that there is an autistic family member.

If you feel like your child would not be able to cooperate in an emergency, there are even decals to place on your car window that lets the paramedics know in an accident that this person may be combative if scared and unresponsive. However, weigh the likelihood of a car accident against the very real threat that a potential predator can see that decal and think, "Hmm, a child who cannot call out for help or report me." Your efforts to keep your child safe just might backfire.

Here's how we protect Carrie as much as we can in situations where she cannot help herself:

1. When we go to a place like an amusement park or crowded event, we still use the accordion-rope bracelets that parents have for youngsters. She might look a little weird, but hey, the folks in Orlando don't know me or my business.

2. I have a laminated card similar to the car decal concept, but it's on Carrie's car seat. It has her name on it and alerts the paramedics that she has autism. It also has about eight different phone numbers for them to call for someone to help them with Carrie (mother-in-law, family members, friends). If Carrie isn't actually hurt in the accident, she's going to be really unhelpful due to the shock and fear, and if I can't speak to reassure her or hold her, a meltdown is bound to happen. If her grandmother was there as soon as possible, it would go a long way to helping Carrie deal with the situation which would free the paramedics to get the steering wheel out of my forehead.

3. We did alert the 911 office to Carrie's condition, mostly because she's getting older and stronger. She may actually put up a huge fight if someone wearing fireman's gear entered her room at night. I don't want her traumatized because two people in heavy clothes and Darth Vadarish air helmets pinned her down then carried her by her arms and legs out of the house.

4. We talk A LOT about what to do in an emergency. If your child is verbal enough to understand when to call and when not to call, you can even teach him to dial 911 and lay the phone down. He does not have to be able to interact to get help, and if you've already alerted 911 to the presence of an autistic family member at the address, they will be less likely to think this is a prank or misdial. When you discuss emergencies, though, you have to be prepared to talk about EVERY potential emergency situation under the sun. It's not enough to say, "When you're hurt, call 911." That's how you get to enjoy a visit from the ambulance when your child gets a paper cut. Talk about every possible parameter that constitutes an emergency.

Chapter 13: Moving

Several years ago we were finally ready to buy our dream house. It was perfect. It had everything we wanted, including all of the considerations we had to make for an autistic child, such as a completely fenced in yard, an alarm system to alert us if she left the house, a master bedroom at the edge of the staircase so we could hear her if she got up in the night, and so much more.

The wonderful people who owned our starter home were amazing, letting us stay for months after we purchased our new home so that we could make the move gradually. (It also allowed Ann to finish out the school year in her first school.) The best thing about the situation was that we gave Carrie plenty of time to adjust to the new situation by moving items to the new house slowly and by sleeping there on the weekends to give her a chance to become accustomed to the house. She was able to "get her feet wet," so to speak, without any of the shock involved in suddenly not living in her first home anymore.

Obviously, not everybody can be so lucky. Part of why it worked is we were basically staying in the same town, although we were changing school districts. My husband and I both kept our jobs, we didn't have to change churches or grocery stores or favorite restaurants, or any of the other myriad new things that crop up when a family moves. It also helped a great deal that this house was bigger and had a better yard, better neighborhood, even a better swing set. Carrie absolutely lived for the weekends when we would go sleep at the "upstairs downstairs house," as she called it.

So how exactly are you supposed to handle it when you have to make a dramatic cross-country move, or a move that will mean leaving behind more than just memories (my parents once had to give up our German shepherd when our move took us from a two-story house in the mountains to a three-bedroom apartment in Korea)? The same way you're going to have to handle telling your other kids about it.

You will need to get all your kids excited about the positives involved in the move (and I know, I'm making a huge assumption that this move is a positive thing) by preparing them in advance. Show them pictures online of your new house, of the town, find a list of all the great restaurants and movie theaters. If your autistic child is fixated on books, like Carrie is, get the info on where the library and the bookstores are. If he loves trains, find out where the train depot is. Better yet, can you pull off a short train ride to your new town? Maybe even from just one town over? Get him excited about the possibilities in order to help minimize the anxiety and outright fear.

Set up email and Skype accounts with all of your child's favorite people from your current location so he knows they won't be forgotten. Let him start emailing and webcamming them even before you move away so he can get used to the grainy image on the screen that is now Grandma's face.

If the move isn't so far away that visiting first is impossible, plan a really great trip before the move, one that involves every possible fun experience. Then you'll be able to say, "We're going to live in the town that had the really awesome water slide!" Take him to see his new school, his new playground, his new swimming pool for the summer time, anything that you can think of that will make this move exciting instead of scary.

Here's how we helped Carrie cope with moving to a new house:

1. We let Carrie choose how her bedroom would look. That's why the walls are navy blue and covered with dinner plate-sized white stars. That's also why there's a two-man camping tent in there instead of a bed.

2. In the months leading up to our actual move, I would take a few boxes of things by there every day after work. It was a little disorienting to Carrie to wake up and find things gone, especially on weekends when we would put the girls to bed then load up a truckful of furniture for my husband to drive out to the house. One day, Carrie woke up and the couch was gone! But letting her see that her favorite things were now waiting in the new house helped her be glad to be at

the new location. When you start packing boxes, make sure you assemble some boxes to set aside that will contain vital things, like a favorite book or some favorite clothes. If it's possible and economical enough, go ahead and buy a few duplicate items, like the favorite book or special pillow, to have waiting at the new house so you don't have to wait for the items to be unpacked from a moving van.

3. We had a lot of conversations about how great it was going to be at the new house. "This is where the swing set will be! This is where the computer and the television are going to be!" As logical people, you and I know that the TV is coming with us. But to children, not just autistic ones, there's no guarantee that a new structure will have the same things that an old structure had. Ann actually asked us if we would have dishes at the new house.

Chapter 14: Embarrassing Your Child

Who among us has never been embarrassed by a loving mom or dear old dad? As teenagers, we lived in mortal fear of being singled out and humiliated, especially by our parents, and it was absolutely toxic if the offense happened in front of our peers or friends.

Well, the same is true for your autistic child. Guess how I know that. Yup, I mortified her one day in public. By the time it was over, she had sullenly moved on and I was the one left in tears.

It was Christmastime at the mall, which is rough on any shopper, autistic or not. Carrie found a display table at the edge of the Hallmark store with small porcelain gingerbread houses on them. She noticed when you ring the doorbell, the little lights edging the roof would flash and a tinny electronic music box embedded somewhere in the bowels of the house would beep-out Christmas tunes. So she pressed the first doorbell. When it finished, she pressed the second doorbell, to see if it did the same thing. When that one was done, she pressed the third. I started counting how many of these stupid houses were lined up on the table. Good grief, fifteen? Why, may I ask? Can't we just leave them in the boxes with only one out on display? Apparently that violates both Hallmark Corp.'s and Christmas rules.

Whenever you make any kind of noise over and over in a store a salesperson will inevitably meander over to see if you found everything you're looking for. I explained that Carrie is autistic and would need to press every one of those doorbells. The woman smiled genuinely at Carrie and walked away.

Carrie buried her face in my shirt and refused to look at another gingerbread house. I had mortified her by telling the woman she's autistic.

Now, I very clearly remember telling you at the beginning of this book that we don't have time to play games with political correctness. But in this case, it simply wasn't any of the woman's business that Carrie has autism. Your kid's school needs to know, so does her doctor, so does her babysitter and so does her Sunday school teacher. The saleslady in the mall? Not so much. There's no reason a normal kid couldn't have stood there touching everyone one of those doorbells, and if the Hallmark store didn't want kids to do that, they wouldn't have put all fifteen of the stupid things in easy reach of anybody over two feet tall.

No matter what I did, Carrie was not willing to look at another gingerbread house. I touched all the buttons in fast succession, trying to get her to look at them and laugh. I got down in front of her and told her she could press them as many times as she wanted to. It didn't help. She tugged my hand away from the store and said, "I go home." I cried all the way to the car.

That was a huge lesson for me. Carrie may not seem to be paying attention, but she hears every word. She might not always respond when I talk, but she's in there and she heard it. More importantly, she understood it. I could barely breathe during the entire drive home, racking my brain to think back to all the times over the years I had talked about her like she wasn't there, times I had told people about her condition or her diagnosis or the outcomes we'd learned. And oh my god I had told people she would probably never have a job or be able to live on her own. I had even talked about possibly needing to have her undergo endometrial ablation if she wasn't able to handle keeping herself clean when she had a period. Right in front of her, because I thought she wasn't paying any attention to me.

I was absolutely ashamed of myself, but I had the understanding to learn from that mistake. I'm passing it on to you.

Here is what we learned about Carrie's feelings:

1. She has them. A good fraction of her day is spent in la-la land. Or so it seems, anyway. But she's not. Don't believe me? Try this test. Walk into a room where your autistic child is engrossed in Legos, step on one of them barefooted, and say, "Shit," under your breath. Guess what you're going to hear next?

2. She is no less sensitive than her sister, or anyone else for that matter. Would you walk up to a small cluster of co-

workers and announce that one of the women standing right in front of you had had a miscarriage two months ago? Or that the guy standing to your left has been cheating on his wife for over a year with the woman standing to your right? Obviously not. That's what it's like when we talk about our kids and mistakenly think they aren't paying attention. They're hearing us bad-mouth or gossip, and even worse, they're the subject.

3. That example made me rethink a lot of the ways I've interacted with Carrie. I learned that she's worthy of an explanation, and apologies. I also learned that she can understand far more than I'd been giving her credit for, so directions and requests became more commonplace, replacing the old stand-by, "It's just easier if I do it myself." If there can even be a silver lining from hurting her so much, it's that I now know she is a lot more independent than I'd been giving her credit for.

Chapter 15: Going On Vacation

I'm going to take you on a vacation. You don't know it, of course, and you have no concept of what a vacation is. So picture it. I'm going to get you out of bed very early one morning, throw you in the car without your usual breakfast, march you at lightning speed through a busy airport where you had to stand without any shoes on for a long time. Then I'm going to put you on an airplane that makes noise and vibrates non-stop and doesn't have your Legos on it. Hours later, I'm going to load you into a car to go to a hotel that has the wrong kind of blanket, none of your stuffed animals, and the television channels aren't the right numbers any more. We're going to walk all day long through museums or galleries or you and I are going to lounge beside a swimming pool for hours, even though I know you despise the smell and feel of sunscreen. After several days of inexplicably not getting to eat in your favorite chair and watch your three favorite DVDs, after days of not having any idea where you are and why your books are nowhere in sight, we will finally repeat the loud vibrating voyage and go home. And dammit, you'd better enjoy every minute of it.

Do you want to continue to take memorable family vacations? Then you're going to have to be the one to adapt, not your autistic child. When we flew to Washington, D.C., Carrie's suitcase had no clothes in it, only toys, books, movies, and all of her favorite foods. Yes, part of the fun of vacationing is doing something different, but autistic kids as a general rule suck at enjoying new things. To you and me, vacationing somewhere far away means trying new foods, taking in new sights. To someone who struggles with object permanence, vacation means you just threw away all of my clothes, toys, books, games, pets, classmates, my grandparents, and my house, only to drop me in a hotel suite that is far smaller than our house, and I will never see any of my familiar, comforting objects again.

Carrie now LOVES to go new places. She is thrilled to death to stay in a hotel and especially loves camping trips. Because every time I plan something like this, I prepare her in advance. I also take into account all of the things that both of my girls love. They both love swimming, so when you're online booking a hotel, choose one with a pool (an indoor pool if it's cold outside). Ann thinks room service is the height of elegance, so I make sure to look for a hotel that will let us choose that as an option one night for dinner. You can even select your specific camping spot at a campground online these days, so I always choose one close enough to the bathroom building that I can watch the girls walk over there, but I also make sure it's close enough to the playground that Carrie can go play with her sister while I get the fire going.

This may also seem like common sense, but when you think of a vacation, are you only thinking of how fun it would be for you to sit in a chaise lounge with a great book you've been dying to read? That's what I think of when I think of luxury! Kids hate just sitting. You dragged them halfway across the world to sit. One of the best trips I've ever taken with my kids was to go to a week-long convention close to the beach. I brought a teenaged babysitter for the week, just so I knew my girls would do more than just sit. While I was in workshops for literally just a few hours a day, this wonderful sitter took them to the hotel pool, but also took them to lunch at the fast food place across the street, the Carnivale museum down the block, the hands-on kids' science museum, and more. They were constantly on the go. I would have to call every time I was headed back to our hotel room, just to make sure they were going to be there!

Here's how to make vacations actually be fun, at least for your autistic child:

1. Prepare way in advance. Carrie struggles even still with the concept of time, so she often cried when it wasn't November (because it was June), when we were supposed to go to the movies on Thursday (and it's only Monday), any time any event was coming up. Sadly, we sometimes had to ignore my own advice and never tell her anything up until the moment it was about to happen. But your child might thrive on knowing what's going to happen and when.

2. Using the calendar glove, we've been able to help her visualize when things will take place as we talk about them ahead of time.

3. In your preparations, show your child pictures of your destination on the internet and pictures of the activities you'll be doing when you get there. Show your child the list of restaurants around your hotel and let him pick one to eat at one night, THEN let him sit while you make the reservation by phone and while you explain that you are bringing someone with special needs, if that's important. Print out the menus from some of the places you'll be eating so he can see that they have cheeseburgers in North Dakota, just like you do at home.

4. Get off your high horse. If your entire extended family is going on a once-in-a-lifetime vacation together, the kind where you see people in Disney World wearing matching T-shirts that read, "We're the Jenkins Family," you're going to have to plan for your child to not want to do some of those things. If everyone has reservations to eat at the Moroccan Pavilion in Epcot Center, there's nothing at all wrong with bringing in a cheeseburger meal from McDonalds. In fact, I've not only had to do that, but I've found that the wait staff of a lot of restaurants will be happy to reheat that Happy Meal that I had to buy six hours ago and keep in a lunchbox-sized cooler when I explain who it's for. It's going to taste like crap, but it's the food your child knows. Sadly, I've always found it was people in my own family who put up the biggest fight, saying things like, "Surely they have SOMETHING here she's WILLING to

eat," and "I didn't fly all the way to New York to eat fast food." Are we on vacation to have fun or to teach someone to put up with whatever crap I can dish out at them? Is your autistic child a human being and a member of your family? Then he wants to have fun, too, and he can't do it with curry-laden Chicken Paprikash simmering in front of him if that's not what he eats.

5. Bring along access to some of the comforts of home, like a favorite movie. Call the hotel and find out exactly what channel carries his favorite TV show. Find out where there might be near-by access to eggs if that's what your child eats for breakfast every day. Don't dismiss his wants just because you're on vacation.

6. Take practice vacations. We call going to stay with my parents, "Vacation to Nonna's house." Driving for two hours to see a friend for the day in another city is, "Vacation to Montgomery." The term "vacation" comes to be something commonplace, so that when the time comes for your family's dream vacation to Ireland, it will be less intimidating.

7. I lived for many years in Italy, and it absolutely freaks Carrie out to hear me speak Italian. For a long time she would just stare at me with a pained expression, but now that she's picked up on phrases like, "Hablo espanol," she is developing an understanding of what it means that not everyone in the world speaks English. However, I don't

think she's ready for a trip back to see friends in Italy. After a 17 hour flight each way, two weeks of not understanding a word anyone is speaking might be more than she's capable of. Of course, I think my non-Italian-speaking husband might feel the same way, and if he would feel that way why shouldn't Carrie? Plan your destination with everyone's needs in mind. Don't let autism dictate every trip you'll ever take, but let it be a part of the planning.

8. Live for the fast food. Face it, if you're a smart parent, you don't eat fast food every single day of the week (yeah, I'm judging you, so what?). But if you were to ask your kids what would be the best food ever, they would say, "Chicken McNuggets, every single day!" So what's wrong with letting them have Taco Bell every day for lunch if it's across the street from your hotel? Are you trying to prove a point or have a fun vacation? Yes, you get to enjoy the fancy locally-owned seafood restaurant with the scrumptious fresh scallops. Many kids hate seafood. Why are you doing that to them? Show up at the restaurant, explain to the waiter that you're on vacation and the food in this little bag you're holding is what your kids wanted, then proceed to eat all the expensive scallops yourself. Everyone is happy.

9. Try to keep disruptions to the routine to a minimum. We took a "surprise" vacation for a few days with our girls,

thinking it would be really cool to get to skip a few days of school for a trip. When we returned and school now started for Carrie on a Wednesday instead of a Monday, it really threw her off. Worse, she missed her favorite activity, which happens on Tuesdays. She wasn't able to process the fact that going to Chattanooga was much more fun than library day.

Chapter 16: The Autism Diet

If we love anything in this country, it's a fad diet. We as a country have suffered through the Low Carb fad, the Sugar Busters AND Fat Busters, the Hard Boiled Egg Diet, just to name a few. If it has a totally unreliable and unfounded promise, we've tried it.

So when Auburn University recommended I try the gluten-free, casein-free diet, or GFCF diet, with my daughter, it was a hard sell. Really? You expect me to believe that never giving Carrie a piece of bread ever again for the rest of her life was going to cure her autism? P.T. Barnum said there was a sucker born every minute. I had already "seen it all" when it came to websites offering autism cures. Saunas installed in your home for the low-low price of $20,000 that would sweat out the toxins that were making Carrie autistic, clay powders at only $30 a bag that would draw those same toxins out through her skin as she sat in the bathtub, crystal necklaces, titanium bracelets, you name it, there's a hell-bound jackwagon out there selling it.

But my first research into the GFCF diet showed me a few eye-opening things. First, the websites that the University sent me to did not sell any products. They didn't sell special foods, nutritional supplements, not so much as a cookbook, which in my book already makes you more legitimate than some of the ideas out there. The only thing that was for sale was a paper copy of all the information on the website in case you wanted a portable version of everything you were able to read up there for free, and even then the cost was for the printing and shipping of this binder to your house. Second, they gave a very unexpected explanation of the logic behind the diet: we don't have a clue as to why this diet helps.

From the information I've managed to garner over the years, here it is in a nutshell. Many people with celiac disease who happened to also be autistic showed a marked improvement in their autistic behaviors when they went on the diet for celiac disease. The thinking is that these patients are not able to process the proteins gluten and casein very well, and that the brain responds to those proteins by dumping chemicals from the brain that impair the patients.

The very first thing this means to you is that it is not going to help every autistic person, only the ones who are not fully able to process those proteins. The second thing you should understand is that it will not hurt your child to give it a try. If your child is an older patient, it might be a little difficult, and I've known parents who had to stop because their children were literally starving themselves. Carrie was two when we began the diet, so she wasn't yet so set in her routine that it was impossible to follow.

Thanks to some celebrities and so-called specialists who shall remain nameless, mostly because there's no damn point in dragging them into this, more than a few parents really believed that if their children never ate a pudding cup ever again, they would be cured.

I'm so sorry. That is just not true.

Carrie has been on the GFCF diet since she was two. She is just as autistic as the day we first found out. However, there are certain behaviors that were greatly improved, mostly things like her verbal skills and her ability to interact with us.

I do NOT want to sound like a snake oil salesman, because I have already stated that this diet is not a cure. It might, however, be a great tool in your autism woodshed. When we began the diet with Carrie, she cried for a day or two. Her routine was interrupted and she probably felt a little weird, just like you or I would if we suddenly ate nothing but scrumptious-but-spicy Middle Eastern food all of a sudden for several days in a row. But on the third day of the diet, Carrie toddled over to the fridge and put all of the number magnets in order; the ten magnet was actually two separate pieces, a yellow 1 magnet and a yellow 0 magnet, as opposed to the regular 1 magnet, that was a stand-alone red one. Huh, intriguing. On the fifth day, Carrie put all of the alphabet magnets in order. I was freaked out, kind of like that scene in *Poltergeist* where the mother comes in the kitchen and all of the chairs are hanging upside down from the ceiling. I scrambled the magnets several times and had her show me again. Then I lost it when

Carrie put all of the vowels across the top in order. I was tempted to think, "Well, the consonants are red and the vowels are all green," right up until she put the red Y up there, too. I began calling neighbors over to come see this, just to make sure it was really what was happening.

The diet did not suddenly make Carrie brilliant. It did not cause her to become a genius. And although we now know she is really bright, it's not like she was a future Mensan trapped inside this body. What most likely happened was Carrie, at age three, had been hearing the alphabet all during the time our family worked with Ann throughout preschool and kindergarten, and the diet helped ease the fog that was keeping her from giving a damn. When she finally wasn't walking around in a natural chemically-induced haze brought on by the foods her system couldn't tolerate, happy just to sit in the floor and flap her hands, she had the energy to stand at the fridge and fiddle with all the magnets.

Whether or not the diet is going to make your child improve, here is actually the biggest endorsement for the diet. It just makes Carrie feel better. I wouldn't care if she talked, wrote novels, became an architect, whatever, as long as I knew she was happy and healthy. And this is what we saw:

Our family was at a large outdoor patio party. From across the very crowded space, I saw Carrie grab a chocolate chip cookie off the buffet table. My heart sank, since I knew there was no way

I could get to her in time to get that cookie out of her grabby little hands. Then I saw the strangest thing. Carrie walked around with the cookie in her claw until she found me. She held it up and asked, "This is for Carrie?" I responded with, "No, that is yucky for Carrie." She handed it to me, wiped her hands on the front of her dress, and took off to play. At four years old she was able to WILLINGLY hand over a cookie and go without one because she understood that the cookie was going to make her feel like crap.

We've noticed that when Carrie accidentally got gluten (wheat, oats, rye, et al), she acted very goofy or loopy. When she ate any milk products, she cried from the physical pain of the headache it produced, coming to me and rubbing her hairline while really crying. That's a very powerful testament to letting her only eat foods found on the GFCF diet.

I made a lot of mistakes with the diet when we first began. The first mistake was in going "cold turkey" off the foods that Carrie was supposed to avoid. I had ordered a great book called *Special Kids, Special Diets*, but before it arrived I just cut out all of these foods. It helped a lot that Carrie was so young, but an older child may have really reacted badly to the sudden loss of not only comfort foods, but to the feelings they used to get from the "bad" foods suddenly being ripped away. I hear crystal meth withdrawal is just as bad.

My second mistake was thinking that I had to "replace" all of the foods that were now verboten with substitutes. I spent hundreds of dollars online ordering soy cheese and rice flour hamburger buns. I would literally carry a special rice hamburger bun with me to McDonalds and supervise them putting her little hamburger together so I could be sure there was no crumb cross-contamination.

Then Carrie would rip the really gross tasting bun apart to get it off her hamburger patty and just eat the meat.

A lot of the foods that are out there for GFCF diets are really nasty. Now, I did not say all of them, I said a lot of them. But think logically. If you're on the GFCF diet because your intestines will blow up and cause internal bleeding if you eat wheat, you're going to learn to get over the aftertaste pretty quickly. Also, if you didn't discover you had this condition until you were a full-blown card carrying adult, you're going to miss cake donuts even more than if you had never eaten many of them. For some people they will need the substitute foods, but many of the autistic kids will not even care.

The easiest thing about the GFCF diet was going to restaurants, which I first panicked about. I didn't realize it was as easy as it is to get Carrie fed, and well fed, at any number of restaurants. Our easiest meals are from buffet-style restaurants, especially Chinese, because there are plenty of raw and basic foods like shredded carrots, hard-boiled eggs from the salad bar, plain white rice, and more. You will have to watch out for sneaky sources of things like butter and milk in these foods, but you can usually find these things out by asking to talk to someone in the kitchen.

Here are some foods your child cannot have if you try the GFCF diet. Anything made out of anything that resembles bread or cake. Anything containing milk, dairy, or butter, or basically began life near a cow.

Here are some foods your child can still eat, although every child may have different degrees of sensitivity (you will have to experiment and possibly add back or cut out specific foods if they don't work out). McDonalds French fries (go online and read all the major companies, since some of them use milk or wheat to form them), movie theater popcorn without the extra butter, many, many types of potato chips from right off the shelves of your regular grocery store, most brands of hotdogs, many different breakfast cereals, a lot of different snack foods, and more.

If you successfully implement the GFCF diet, you might find that your whole family eats healthier. I don't mean that you must force your entire family onto this anti-gluten kick, although there is currently a popular movement to cut back on some of the gluten in our diets. What I found was that I prepare meals now that are so much simpler than before. Each dinner contains a very basic protein source, say grilled chicken, with a little barbecue sauce on the side since Carrie doesn't like the overwhelming flavors in it, one or two steamed vegetable side dishes (again, salt and/or parmesan cheese is on the table to be added individually to keep it off of Carrie's plate), and some nights one of the vegetable side dishes might be replaced with a rice or potato side, but not every night. Once you begin cooking this way for one family member, you'll find that most of your meals become simple and tasty, rather than the elaborate casseroles and involved recipes of the past.

This is not to say that you can't have a meatloaf anymore, you would just need to make sure you kept aside some of the basic ingredients to assemble a meal for your GFCF family member.

Which brings me to another huge mistake we made when implementing this diet, which was to behave as though we couldn't eat certain foods in front of Carrie. We could never eat pizza in front of her again, or have that meatloaf, because she would be upset. When we finally caved a little, I used to have my husband bring home a Happy Meal (ordered without the bun or toppings), so she could eat that and "feel special" while we ate meatloaf. First, Carrie wasn't the slightest bit concerned with what was on our plates, and second, Ann really wanted to know why she wasn't eating McDonalds.

Over time, we got over it. Carrie eats her foods and she's happy, we eat our foods and we're happy. She doesn't look around at our plates and sigh resignedly. Sometimes, just for fun, when we eat pizza I'll make Carrie a pretend pizza out of mashed potatoes smeared with ketchup and a few pepperoni placed on top. She laughs and eats it, getting the joke that this looks like a pizza. If I buy her a special $6 GFCF mini rice-crust pizza with soy cheese on top that I had to drive an hour each way to buy for her, she may or may not eat it.

Here are some things that helped Carrie with the GFCF diet:

1. Read up all you can about this diet before deciding if it's something your family wants to implement. Understand that, from what I have read about the diet, there is no cheating. Once you let your child have a little bite of cookie, you just blew it. You will have to start over and go through "cookie detox" all over again. It's not like calories where you can make it up later.
2. When we went cold turkey, we basically threw Carrie onto a low-carb diet. Her weight plummeted, which was very scary. Get all your information before you do anything else. There are great websites (gfcfdiet.com, allergygrocer.com, just to give you two) and books out there, including the ones that address gluten-free/casein-free from the standpoint of being the parent of a normal child who has celiac disease. There is even a celiac disease foundation who can give you a lot of information.

3. Decide how long you are going to try this diet to see if it "works." We set a completely arbitrary limit of one month, mostly because we were starting this at the very end of November and if it wasn't going to work for Carrie, we didn't want it to interfere with Christmas holiday meals with family. During that first month we saw some improvement, so we kept extending the time limit to two months then to three months, because even we weren't willing to claim it was "working" when it really was. It was too easy.

4. Be prepared for things like how you're going to handle birthday parties at school (they email me and tell me when I need to send something for Carrie), trick-or-treating (there are plenty of candy varieties out there that GFCF kids can eat), holiday dinners at relatives' houses, etc.

5. Lastly, decide if the extra effort is producing a result that is worth it. As I said, this was basically Carrie's choice. She is eight years old now and still will not eat a new food unless I tell her it's okay. If it never did anything for her in terms of bringing out her intelligence or social ability (both of which were things that we did see), it obviously makes her feel so much better and her health is in no way jeopardized.

Chapter 17: Dealing With Unsupportive Relatives

With any luck, my mother-in-law will never read this book. And neither will my parents. Or my coworker. Or even the nurse at our regular physician's office who rolls her eyes when I say, "No, it's not time for more shots yet." Or any of the other people who have either been unsupportive, uncaring, or just downright foot-in-their-mouths stupid, either intentionally or purely by dumb-luck accident.

It is somewhat embarrassing and shameful to admit that my husband and I did not see eye-to-eye on the issue of Carrie receiving Early Intervention Therapies. My husband somehow got it worked up in his mind that since we were not going to be billed for these services and since the program was funded by the federal government, it was akin to welfare. And we were not going to accept welfare. I was absolutely dumbfounded.

He seriously made me call around to various speech therapists, occupational therapists, physical therapists, to our insurance company, and more, trying to find out how to get referrals, how much it would cost to have them work with her, and how we could be seen as private patients. To say they laughed at me isn't exactly accurate, it was more like all of these people were completely confused by what I was asking.

When I finally reported to my husband that it wasn't possible to make these appointments without a doctor's referral, and that these therapists couldn't even tell me how much they earned per hour because it just doesn't work that way, he was irritated with me for not doing a better job of gathering the information. I finally made one last inquiry phone call: to a divorce attorney. I let my husband know in absolutely no uncertain terms that if he stood in the way of Carrie receiving the help she needed, I would leave him. Furthermore, the consultation with the lawyer showed me that if I had to leave my husband because he was preventing Carrie from receiving medical care, he wouldn't even get visitation of either daughter, let alone any form of custody.

I would love to tell you that my determination helped open his eyes to just how grave the situation was. No, instead, he told me I could do whatever I wanted, just not to ever even talk to him about it. Carrie and I worked through two years of Early Intervention without so much as a, "How's she doing?" from my husband. You know, the guy who is Carrie's biological father but who still wouldn't do whatever it took to get her help.

It would be awesome if that was the only hurdle I had to face. My in-laws were convinced there was nothing wrong with her and I heard about that a lot. My parents' pendulum swung in the other direction, to the point that I had to inform them that I had a life before autism came along and that I was going to devote at least ten minutes a day to doing something besides talk about autism. They were also sometimes fond of pointing out that I'm not doing nearly enough for Carrie, since I have not quit my job, sold my house, and moved her to a major city that had a great preschool program for autistic kids.

I personally know one parent who had to make the soul-destroying decision to institutionalize her autistic son at the age of nine. You would not believe the venom that can spew from the mouths of people you thought you cared about until you have to face a decision like that one. Some of the morsels people actually spoke to this parent's face make me ashamed to be a member of the human race. Comments about how she must not have wanted this one after all, and about how she's keeping the other two "perfect" children and shoving this one in a closet…it just gets worse from there. The fact that this woman is allowed to see her son twice a month, once when he gets to come home for a weekend and once when she makes the hour drive to see him for the day, that negates any right ANYONE else on the planet has for speaking to her about this. For a hospital staff member to look me in the face and say, "It's just too upsetting for your son when you show up for an unplanned visit," would be the end of my life, and anyone who has something snarky to say about it had best make sure I don't overhear it or there will be bloodshed.

So what do you do when your elderly grandmother talks about how in her day kids "like that" went to go live in homes? Or when your sister-in-law wants to know why your son STILL isn't potty trained, since all of her children and all of his cousins and every child everywhere on the planet was already potty trained by this age? Or when your own spouse wants to get pissed at you because your autistic child grabs herself between the legs when she's scared and "it's just disgusting," what then, huh?

First, refuse to be second-guessed. Make a proclamation from the rooftop if you must. You have my permission to tell any and all sundry friends and relatives that if they are not on board, they are not welcomed to interfere or suggest.

Second, be prepared to fight this battle for the rest of your life. After some time, it will become second nature to tell staring strangers who suggest that "that child just needs a good whipping" during a tantrum that you know quite a few bossy adults who could use a good ass-kicking, too.

Third, convince yourself of this fact. Ninety-nine percent of the time, those comments or second-guesses are TRULY because the person speaking them cares so much but doesn't have a clue what to do for you. If you fell down dead in front of me, I would begin CPR. If your arm spontaneously fell off your body, I would pack it in ice to bring to the hospital while applying a tourniquet to your stump made from my own bra. But I don't have a clue what to do for you if you walk up to me and say, "My three-year-old has leukemia," except grab you in a bear hug, tell you I will pray for your child every hour on the hour, and hopefully not say something monumentally stupid. There are some things even I can't fix and these morons are no different.

I choose to believe that the confrontations I endured are because the speaker truly wanted to make sure I was doing the best I could for Carrie, and it's easy to believe because the biggest battles I've faced have been from Carrie's own grandparents. I know mothers-in-law are such an easy target for jokes, but I know mine loves me and my entire family with every scrap of her soul. If we were all trapped in a burning building, my mother-in-law would throw herself out of the third floor window and let us land on her squishy body to cushion our falls. She wants nothing more than the absolute happiness of her grandbabies, especially Carrie.

So when she would nag about the diet, or argue, or tearfully ask us AGAIN why we wouldn't let Carrie eat chicken McNuggets, we would have to just grit our teeth and patiently explain AGAIN that this is what's best. Sometimes we would have to resort to saying, "This is just what we're going to do." I don't think she ever did agree that the diet is helpful for Carrie and I know she has OFTEN flat-out told me she doesn't think it's good for her; of course, it doesn't help that Carrie is naturally a skinny little kid and all grandmothers in America think their grandchildren are starving to death.

Here's what you can do to help your various friends and relatives be helpful:

1. Stand your ground. You know that you are doing all you can. It might not be what other people would do, but it's what you and your family have decided is right in your situation.

2. Do listen to their comments. Advice is free, it didn't cost you anything but time to listen to. But don't let people belittle you or cause you to question yourself.

3. Give IMPORTANT people in your lives (ie, the grandparents, your best friend whose kids live next door and who like to play with your kids all the time) the ability to be helpful. My mother-in-law LOVES to ply the grandbabies with sugar, which irks the snot out of me, but am I really going to fight her on this? She lives thirty miles away, it's not a daily occurrence. The planet isn't going to blow up if your kid eats six marshmallows while you're trying to fill his plate at a family dinner. I've given her a list of every food that Carrie can have at her house, including Frito-Lay corn chips, Pillsbury brand white icing, and Haagen Das strawberry sorbet, just so she can keep these foods handy to shovel into my kids' mouths. It helps her feel like she gets to be a doting grandmother instead of an outsider who's going to do something wrong. Help these people to be a positive part of your autistic child's life instead of the enemy.

4. There's a subtopic to this section, called: (keep reading)

Chapter 18: Visiting Family

Going to see family is no less stressful than going on vacation and all of the considerations from any vacation still apply. Sadly, many visits to family mean you will need a vacation when it's over. Even more so than a regular vacation, seeing family members may carry with it certain expectations from you and from your relatives and some of these may be expectations that your autistic child can't meet. Have you noticed that the first day you're there it's a big game of catching up followed by a few hours of reminiscing, but by day 1.5 some of you are starting to make snarky comments and criticize? Be prepared for the remarks about what you're doing right or wrong as a parent of an autistic child. I have actually had to tell my own family members, "No offense, but you don't know what you're talking about," when it came time to defend my parenting strategies or explain why certain things were done a certain way.

Here's how we handle the conflicts that can come up when visiting family:

1. Resist the urge to hold up a gloved hand at your mother and tell her you will stir the noodles when the timer beeps.
2. Do let your parents see you utilizing the techniques in your arsenal. We have cousins who absolutely plotzed themselves when they realized I had given Carrie

permission to "touch herself" as long as she did it in the bathroom. She was lying on the floor with her face pressed against the hardwood, very stressed out by all the loud talking relatives, televisions blaring sports games, and smells coming from the kitchen, when I noticed her hand had traveled south. I leaned over and said, "If you need to do that, it's more polite to go into the bathroom." You would have thought I recommended that she choose Exotic Dancer as a career path. I did end up having to firmly tell those cousins that they are not to make her feel ashamed, ever again.

3. Keep in mind that your relatives are probably not raising an autistic child, so while you are within your rights to sweetly tell them that you've got it under control without superfluous advice, always remember that they are hurting for you and for your struggle to do a great job. My parents would literally take their own lives if it could help my daughter and sometimes in their efforts to be helpful they can say or do things that are not quite as useful as they think. Remember that they love you and want to do whatever they can. If that's not the case, why the hell are you visiting these people?

Chapter 19: Navigating Preschool And School

Guess what? Your child isn't special. That hurt, didn't it? The rest of the world doesn't think your child is any more special than anyone else's child. And that's how it should be. If the entire world thought that every single child was the most precious thing on the planet, there would be no need for parents. Your child has a mom and a dad because someone has to give a damn about him more than they do about all the other kids. Caring about your child's needs first is your job, not the school's job. The school's job is to care about the needs of some five hundred children on a daily basis. When you understand that, you will have an awesome relationship with your child's school.

Let me tell you a story about trying to return some running shoes. Once upon a time, I bought some extremely expensive running shoes as a Mother's Day present to myself. This story does not involve the reasons why I had to buy my own present. I had worn this style and brand of running shoes for years and was just getting a new pair of the same exact shoes. Somehow, when it came time to actually purchase the shoes, I had put the wrong size in the wrong box. I gave back the ones that actually fit me and took the wrong size with me to the register.

It took two months of running in these horrible shoes to figure out that they were the wrong size. Sometime in July, I gathered up the shoes and took them back to the major-chain fitness store where I'd bought them. The cutie behind the counter at customer service asked if she could help me, and this is how it played out:

"I reeeeeally hope you can help me, but if you can't I TOTALLY understand. I have these shoes that I bought here on Mother's Day, you know, two months ago. I don't have the box, the tags, or the receipt, but I somehow got the shoes swapped and I bought the wrong size. I've been running in them this whole time. Is there anything at all you can do for me, maybe just even a teensy little discount towards another pair?" I cringed in anticipation. The cutie replied, "Of course we'll exchange them! Just throw them right here in this pile and go get yourself a brand-new pair from the back."

By going into that store with a humble attitude, the utmost in politeness, and a willingness to admit that the sales girl's hands might be tied, I walked out with a brand-new pair of shoes to replace the ones that I was stupid enough to buy AND run in for two months in the first place. Kill 'em with kindness, my mama used to say. And I'm not bragging that I manipulated these people in any way, I'm telling you that my attitude towards the situation resulted in the customer service girl wanting to be helpful in the first place. If I'd gone in there acting like a jerk, she would have been well within the company policy to tell me I was up the creek.

That very same approach goes into dealing with your child's school. Unless they are absolute morons, which has been known to happen in the world of special ed, they want the best for your child. Sadly, they don't have a counterfeit money operation set up in the basement of the school. You want an aide for your child? You want assistive technology because he doesn't write or read well? You want the IEP meeting scheduled at YOUR convenience, no matter that the six other people who are required by law to attend had to jump through your dog-and-pony show hoops to be there and that most of them had to find substitute teachers to cover their classes so you could spout your list of demands? I've said it before: get over yourself.

Just because your child's school is required by law to educate your child and to do it to the best of their abilities does not mean for a second that your state and federal governments are giving them the funds and tools to do it. The last thing they need, and the one thing that will keep them from bending over backwards to help your child be successful in school, is your pissy attitude.

The cost of this book will be more than made up for if you don't take anything else away from it but this: if you ever say the word lawsuit, you just became the enemy. I do not mean to imply for a minute that there is not a legitimate and vital reason for suing your child's school system, but as a parent and as a teacher, if I had a dime for every time I heard a parent of any child threaten to call a lawyer, or even better, to spout that stupid phrase, "I pay your salary with my taxes," my child's financial future would be secure. You know what? I'm a teacher and I pay my taxes, too, so basically by that logic I pay my own salary which makes me my own boss. So shut up and go away.

These people didn't become special ed teachers because of the massive NFL-style signing bonus. They don't work at the school because it's the one place where they could get their name spray-painted on a parking spot. The teachers at my child's school are required to report for work each morning at 6:35! My children are not out of bed at 6:35, but these teachers (and their own children, by the way) are there, dressed and groomed and ready to greet the day. They are not the enemy.

They are one of the few factions of people on the planet who think your very special child deserves all the help there is. If you hopped on down to Walmart and asked people in the parking lot if they would be willing to give up eight hours of their days and a good chunk of their income to educate your child, be prepared for the riot of laughter. But the people at your child's school, at least in the beginning, chose this career because they really wanted to be a voice for your baby.

My only complaint with the special ed department at my child's school has been that they let her get by with murder. All she has to do is crawl up in her aide's lap, bat her eyes, and say, "Awwww, you make me so happy," and she doesn't have to a) do schoolwork, b) run laps in PE class, or c) go to the principal's office for screaming at people. I've had to order them to stop letting her wrap them around her little finger.

And it happens that way because we are good parents at that school. We are there for every event, we support every fund raiser, we volunteer when we can and send in money or supplies whenever a situation warrants. In a perfect world it wouldn't come down to which parents send in the most money and support, but look at it from their point of view. As a teacher, I've personally called my students' parents to talk to them about their children's behavior or schoolwork, only to hear, "Why the f*ck are you calling me at my house?" Go figure, the parents who show a modicum of support and are willing to meet the school halfway, the ones who are willing to actually READ the notes that get sent home and offer up suggestions for what has worked and what has not, those are the people whose children succeed, special needs or not.

So how do you go about creating this educational nirvana? First, adopt the attitude that you are entitled to absolutely nothing from these people, that they are not there to serve the needs of your child and your child alone. Then you will be pleasantly shocked by all they do for you. Let me describe my daughter's day:

Carrie's morning aide is waiting outside of the school for her, rain or shine, sunny day or thirty below zero. Instead of having to wait through the car-rider drop-off line, I'm permitted to pull over, park my car, and carry her in. Now, admittedly, Carrie is afraid the shrubs and gets upset at walking through the doorway, so I'm allowed this special parking arrangement because it helps her. The aide and I walk to Carrie's class with the aide carrying Carrie's backpack, since I'm hefting an 8-year-old child.

I go into the classroom and help Carrie set up her own personal laptop computer, the one she's allowed to use for all of her schoolwork, and I put away her notebook. Her classroom teacher comes over to me and we talk for a few minutes about how Carrie's feeling today, how she slept, if she's having any difficulties with schoolwork, etc. The aide has taken Carrie down the hall to the special ed classroom because Carrie likes to go sign her name on that teacher's white board each morning. Carrie calls it "signing in."

Once I leave for work, Carrie comes back and starts her day with her morning aide sitting beside her, even during PE and recess.

At lunch, all of the students line up to go to the cafeteria, except Carrie. Back in kindergarten we discovered that the cafeteria is a scary place to Carrie. It's full of very loud children, but also the refrigerators emit a constant high-pitched squeal which causes Carrie to cover her ears and cry. So guess where Carrie eats her lunch? In the special ed teacher's classroom. Every year that teacher adjusts her schedule to make sure that she has planning period when Carrie has lunch, just so Carrie can eat her lunch in there, play on the computer, and get some extra one-on-one time. I guess it would actually be two-on-one time, since the aide stays in there throughout the lunch and they both talk, teach, and play with Carrie. This is usually the time of the day that they let Carrie email me from the teacher's computer, so many days I get a personal message from my daughter telling me how her day is going and how much she loves me. Cue the violins.

After lunch, the morning aide goes to help a different student and Carrie's afternoon aide takes over. This is by design so that neither of them gets burned out from working with the same child all day long, day-after-day and so Carrie learns to adapt to different people and not become dependent on the aide. Both paraprofessionals are awesome people and we're thrilled to have them.

After school, Carrie has to go to the after school program until I get off work, which usually means she's there for not quite two hours, since their schools dismiss at 2:20 and mine doesn't dismiss until 3:30, plus travel time. AIDE NUMBER THREE takes over. You heard that right, the third paraprofessional comes each day to watch Carrie during the after school program, because again, she doesn't tolerate the cafeteria and large hordes of noisy children. Just so Carrie doesn't feel isolated and is given plenty of opportunity to be around her normal peers, Carrie, the aide, and a small select handful of other students go to the computer lab to play games.

On the off chance that something prevents the after school aide from being there, you're never going to guess what the official back-up plan is: the principal himself is to watch Carrie. That's right, the principal of the entire school is to fill in for the after school aide. That was his own decision.

Now, you're already thinking I have either won some massive due process lawsuit, or I have naked pictures of somebody on the school board. Neither. I went into this relationship with my daughter's school with a helpful attitude and have yet to stamp my little foot and make demands. You are going to work with these people for approximately thirteen years, you might want to make sure those years are pleasant.

Here are some of the things that we do have academically that have made a lot of difference:

1. Every year when textbooks are issued to the students, I receive a second set to keep at home so that Carrie doesn't have to lug books home in her back pack. This allows me to be on top of what she's learning and helps her to bridge the school-vs-home worlds.

2. In Carrie's IEP, it states that she will not be graded on homework. That one was my only request, because she struggles so hard to behave and be productive for eight hours a day and the last thing I want to do is pile more schoolwork on her at home. Plus, the doctor authorized an entire dose of her medication so she can focus on homework and I'm just not willing to drug her AGAIN to do more schoolwork. Her school heartily agreed. They still send it home with her so I can see what she's working on in school and I can talk with her about it; even better, if she is having a great day for focusing and actually does the homework, she still gets a grade on it, but if she doesn't do it, she is not penalized.

3. I'm not a big dreamer. I know full-well that Carrie qualifies for an aide throughout the school day because she struggles with elopement issues, meaning that she will run off at any time. She was actually picked up by the police one Sunday when we turned out backs for just a split second. I also know the funding isn't there to keep these aides just to help her with academics, but she qualifies for them because of her safety issues. We keep the school informed of every

single instance in which she attempts to flee, because at the end of the school year they are the ones who have to justify why the system is spending money on these people.

4. There is no such thing as giving your child's school or teacher too much information when it comes to letting them know things. I have been enraged by parents who finally sit down with me in November for a conference, only to have them admit that their child is supposed to be taking Ritalin but they haven't stopped by the pharmacy in two months to get it for him. In those cases, I couldn't produce the Ritalin the child needed, but I certainly could have tried some classroom strategies to help a child who is off his meds, IF the parents had bothered to inform me. Everything from how tired she is, to how cranky she's been, to letting them know that certain holidays or movies tend to upset her, there's no such thing as useless information.

Chapter 20: Siblings

The person I am the most sad for, the person I still cry myself to sleep over sometimes, isn't my autistic daughter. It's her sister. Ann really got the shaft when it comes to siblings. She was only two years old when I was pregnant with Carrie and throughout my pregnancy this angel had it all planned out in her head. She talked about how they were going to watch movies together, how they were going to share a room and get bunk beds when they were big enough. And I got sucked in, too. I had visions of Ann telling her sister all about how her date went, about Ann and Carrie reading books in the hammock in the back yard, about them sharing clothes and Carrie following Ann everywhere trying to be just like her big sister. From the moment I found out the baby was going to be a girl, I could see it all. And that's not what happened. Every time Ann even touched her baby sister, Carrie would arch her back and scream.

Now, Ann is in middle school and has to serve as her sister's lookout. Ann is the "sister of the retard." Ann lives and breathes for her sister and that's not right. She's supposed to argue over whose turn it is to sit in the front seat or pick which movie we watch, not gladly hand over her dessert just because her sister used a complete sentence when she asked for it. Ann is a sucker for her sister's hugs and Carrie knows it.

If your child is not an only child, chances are good that you have some kids in your household who often feel pushed aside and insignificant. Even worse, they may feel resentful of their siblings at times, which is compounded by the feelings of guilt they have for feeling anything less than worshipful love towards their autistic brother or sister.

I read a FABULOUS book called *Rules* by Cynthia Lord (Scholastic). It is a young adult fiction book and it's all about a junior high school-aged girl whose younger brother is profoundly autistic. It was a work of such bleak despair and eye-opening pain that I finished it in one sitting. I closed the cover when I finished, and my only thought was, "Oh God, please don't let me have done that to Ann." Throughout the book, you are treated to an inside view of how hard it is on the entire family to have a child with autism in the home. The mother started working from home years ago in order to homeschool her child because her son couldn't "behave" in school, so all of the responsibility for her son's care falls to the older sister from the moment she walks in the door from school, freeing Mom up to handle her work-related business. The father works overtime every day so they can afford all of the expensive therapies they need for their son, so he comes home exhausted and unwinds in his vegetable garden, too tired to talk or help with homework or even drive the sister to a friend's house. Even worse, money is tight. One scene in particular broke my heart: the sister, who is a good artist, asked for a new colored pencil from the art shop to replace one that was worn down, but the mother said they couldn't afford it right then. When the sister finally caved in to her feelings of resentment and argued, "You'd buy it if it was for David," her mother actually said, "That's different."

I was mortified, not at the subject matter of the book but at the possibility that we had done it to Ann. How many times had Ann had to change the channel on the television during one of her shows because Carrie was screaming and the only way to calm her down was to put on her favorite DVD? How often had I made Ann "help your sister," essentially saying to her, "Whatever you're doing isn't as important as whatever your sister is doing," and not only that, but that I was too important or lazy to help Carrie myself?

Here are some of the ways we make sure that we are as fair as we can be to both of our children:

1. We instituted an "account" for Ann, which is basically just a spare checkbook register. Whenever I ASK (note that, ask, not tell) her to do something outrageous for her sister (ie, change the channel during her movie, stop what she's doing because Carrie wants to play Yahtzee AGAIN) or basically anything that smacks of unfairness, Ann gets a dollar in her checkbook register. That way, I'm not actually handing over cash on a daily (hourly) basis, but Ann can

see that I know this isn't fair so I'm trying to compensate her. When Ann wants something outside of the ordinary at the store (black nail polish, a ticket to the movies when I hadn't budgeted to take us to the movies), she can use what is built up in her register.

2. More importantly, with the checkbook register, there is choice. "If you will stop and play Hungry, Hungry Hippos AGAIN, I'll put a dollar in your register." "I really want to just finish my book." "Okay then." End of discussion. Ann has NEVER once told me she would not do something for Carrie, and I believe it's all because I gave her the choice to do it. I didn't order her to do while her sister screamed, which would breed resentment. I offered her the option to do it for compensation, albeit ridiculously little compensation, but that one dynamic clearly says to Ann, "I realize that this isn't fair to you and I'm willing to provide you with this money because of it." Most of the time Ann will tell me that I don't even have to pay her...

3. ...which brings us to teaching your normal children to stand up for themselves. They will be far more likely to defend an autistic sibling at school if they feel your support for their feelings at home.

4. Do not be afraid to reward your normal children or be a little over-the-top for them sometimes. The demands that Carrie places on my time are so great that Ann does appreciate the little things, like when I slip her some candy

that I bought just for her from the store or sneak up behind her with a new book I've bought for her. That gesture in the presentation lets her know, "I did this just for you and even though I didn't get anything for your sister, it's okay because right this moment YOU are the special kid that got all my attention." Before you get irritated, hear me out. Life cannot always be equal; if it was, your normal children would be spending an hour a week with a speech therapist, too. There is absolutely nothing in the world wrong with doing something for one of your children and not the others sometimes, as long as it's happening for all of them in turn. Carrie spends about three hours a week with me when her sister is off at church activities or baton lessons, just this special Mom-time that Ann isn't getting, and since I can't make a day have more hours in it, I have to find ways to make Ann feel just as important as her sister.

5. I have a few relatives who were more than a little pissed about some of the extraordinary ways we choose to find time together as a family. The girls and I will go out of town a lot and my husband will come with us when his schedule allows. There have been family trips to Washington, D.C., multi-day trips to San Francisco, an almost yearly trip to Disney World when we go to Florida to visit some of our family members. And it's not about money, since we are solidly middle class, but about how we choose to spend it. We don't drive brand-new cars or live in

a brick McMansion, which frees up our income to try to make a lot of special times for our kids. There will be plenty of time for life to suck as they get older and older, like when I'm dead and Ann has to visit Carrie in a group home on every major holiday instead of spending it with her own family. Now is the time I can teach them just how important they are to me and how important family is to all of us.

6. When I have to be unfair, I talk it through with Ann. I also try to really pronounce the times that I'm telling Carrie to just deal with it, because Ann needs to hear me stand up for her. Most TV programs scare Carrie, so we had to tell Ann there will be no more Spongebob in the living room. We even got her a small laptop for Christmas so she can live-stream episodes on the laptop in her room. When Carrie walked past Ann's room one day and heard Spongebob playing, she began to scream and demand that it be turned off. I took Carrie into my bedroom, sat her on the bed, and quite loudly explained that Ann is allowed to watch it in her room and Carrie can play somewhere else in the house. It was for Carrie's benefit, but also for Ann's.

Chapter 21: Being Afraid

Every year at the beginning of the school year we fill out page after page of forms about our children, one of them being the classroom questionnaire. This form is for the classroom teacher to get to know her students better. One of the items towards the bottom is always, "Does your child have any fears or anxieties?" That's when I usually have to raise my hand and ask for more paper because those three lines and most of the back of the paper are already filled.

Carrie is afraid of shrubs. Seriously? Shrubs? And television. Not just a few TV shows, but all of them. She's afraid of all fruits and vegetables, which I used to think was just an act to avoid eating healthy foods, but once a carrot is cut up on her plate she's fine with it. If you poke her with it, she screams. You don't want to know how I found that out.

The world your child lives in is scary and confusing. People purposely douse themselves with crazy-smelling chemicals and paint themselves with goop that makes them not look like themselves anymore. Men shave their faces and leave them scratchy. Some people have hair and some don't, for some bizarre reason. Cars are usually quiet but sometimes without warning they will make all kinds of loud scary noises, often causing the people inside the car to make loud and scary noises. Toys that look like they just want to give you a hug will suddenly light up and start shaking and when it makes you cry, the grown-ups in the room laugh. Soda bottles sit quietly on the countertop but when you want a drink of root beer, someone turns the top and it makes a loud hissing noise like an angry snake and if you were in a hurry when you opened it, the root beer might fly all over the kitchen for no reason. This is one screwed up world we live in.

Here are some of the ways we've tried to help Carrie be less afraid:

1. Make concessions for it. Ann is forbidden to watch Spongebob downstairs because it scares the bejeebuz out of Carrie, so she must watch it in her room. It's allowed to be on, but it doesn't have to be on in the main part of the house where you can't help but see it. This works on several levels because the sound of that stupid little invertebrate's voice makes my teeth itch.

2. After making some concessions, there's nothing wrong with trying to teach your child to deal with it. We do not live in a Spongebob-free Zone, we just limit it to certain locations. We did not rip all the shrubs out of the front of our house, but we don't keep houseplants inside. However, I don't avoid the garden department of Lowe's. Carrie can hunker down in the shopping cart all she wants to, if it's the fastest route to the car in the rain, that's the way we're going.

3. I purposely set up scenarios that will introduce Carrie to some of her fears but in a controlled way. There are tons of movies she's scared of, but every so often I will lock her in my bedroom with me and play a little bit of some of these movies. I use the glove to show her how long she has to watch it, and I'll even hit MUTE to start out with it. When she finally calms down and shows a little interest in the movie, I will tell her that I'm going to turn it up just a tiny bit so I can hear it, but still keeping it barely audible. Next time, watch a little longer and a little louder. You might wonder why I would do that to her, but basically it's because she's missing out on some things in life due to her self-imposed fears. I'm sorry, but *Finding Nemo* is a darn cute little movie and I want her to see it. That was the first one we force-watched together and when she calmed down and actually watched the screen for a while, she talked about it with me. She asked the shark's name, and what were they looking for, and why was that little fish taken away and put in a fish tank. That's a big deal and it wouldn't have happened if I didn't try to force Carrie to face some of her fears.

4. Some fears may seem irrational, but if you pay close attention you can get to the bottom of it. Carrie is afraid of shrubs because she was stung by a bee while standing next to our camellia bush. Normal people would hate bees, but since it happened by the bush, Carrie hates bushes. To help

her overcome that, we talk a lot about how pretty that bush is or how nice that tree looks. We sniff every damn plant in the garden department, just to practice standing with our faces close to nature.

5. At the same time, just because there was a logical introduction to the fear, that doesn't mean it can be allowed to continue unchecked. Do what you can in baby steps and tiny doses to help your child overcome his fears.

Chapter 22: Faith

If your religious views aren't in line with mine, I completely understand and respect your beliefs. I happen to be a mainstream Christian, and by that I mean I am of one of the more widespread denominations in this country. Therefore, I would like to say, if you feel that you want to skip over this chapter, I respect your choice. However, no matter what your religious views, whether you believe in God or Allah or Vishnu or karma or no higher power, you might still glean a healthy outlook by reading these pages. I will not be using them to preach to anyone, but if you should find yourself more interested in learning about a faith, yours, mine, or any of the ones out there, I would encourage you to do so within your community.

Having said that, I will be referring to God in this chapter because that is what I believe, but it would not offend me if you substituted your own belief in a higher power in His place. But I urge you to read on.

It is a hard fact to wake up every day knowing that God did this to me and to my family, my beautiful autistic child included. Life would have been so much easier if autism had not reared its head in my family. But really, there are no guarantees that anything would have been easier.

So here it is: you have hit rock bottom as a parent the day you pray to God to ask Him help you love your child. I didn't pray for Him to make her normal or make her autism be less severe than some of the other kids I knew. At the point, I wasn't even up to praying for her future. I was right there face down on the ground, crying, praying that there never be a day that I am bitter or resentful or that I blame her for the mess my family finds itself in. You are the lowest human on the planet when you're not absolutely certain you can love your baby, and there I was.

So I never got around to praying for Carrie to learn to talk or go to college or live independently. I promised God that if He would provide love at all times, I would do my job and I would do it without complaint. Just please don't let me hate her, ever.

A lot of my fellow Christians have asked me how I can be so upbeat and have such a funny personality, as if having Carrie destroyed my ability or my right to laugh. Half the time, I'm laughing at something she said or did, because she's a really smart, funny person. One of the core beliefs of my religion is that God is at work in all things, so therefore by scripture, that would mean God is at work in my family's life. Who am I to be sad, then?

There was one specific Sunday during our church service where I started crying so borderline-hysterically that my husband leaned down to ask in a whisper if I needed to leave. I wasn't crying because of my situation in life, but because of the words to one of the songs the choir was singing, words that were taken straight from Scripture: "My name is graven on His hand."

When I'm working on a book or a project, I often write important things on my hand in Sharpie so it won't wash off. Carrie's name is written on the hand of God. When He looks down throughout His day, he sees my child's name. Who am I to worry? How dare I be concerned about her future in light of that? That one image of my child's name carved in the hand of God has brought me more peace than anything anyone on Earth has been able to say or do for me.

As a logical person, I would love for God to personally tell me what the point of all this was. I've also come to accept that the chances of that happening aren't all that great. I have had to consciously teach myself to look for the moments when I think Carrie's diagnosis is being used for the universal good. For example,

There Has To Be A Point To All This #1: Carrie was featured in a five minute ad for our state's public broadcasting affiliate. Camera crews came to my home and interviewed me about how Carrie connects with the public television programming, then shot footage of Carrie watching all of her favorite PBS television shows. Guess when they love to show this one? During their fundraising telethons. Cue the beautiful blonde baby who learned to speak thanks to Sesame Street. The whole point was to get people to think, "Awwww, where's my checkbook?" and I'm fine with that. PBS needs all the support it can get and Carrie really does love those shows. If featuring her on one of their segments makes politicians vote to keep public television available to children in the housing projects, all the better.

There Has To Be A Point To All This #2: Ann had a classmate in kindergarten who was profoundly autistic. Mitch wasn't diagnosed, though, until his second year in kindergarten. His parents were not highly educated and were very young when they had him; on top of that, he was their first child, so the strange behaviors they saw really didn't register as weird. By the time Ann became his classmate, he had already failed his first year of school.

Because Ann was very familiar with the behaviors she saw from Mitch, she didn't really think anything of them. Even though we had never had a sit-down discussion with Ann to tell her that there was anything wrong with her sister, she was already attuned to the quirks Mitch displayed. This tolerance on her part made her the only child who would sit next to Mitch, the only one who would play with the "weird kid." Even the teacher, who was as sweet as they come, would have to ask Ann to translate what Mitch was trying to say from time to time. Mitch's mom let me know that Ann was Mitch's only friend. In the world.

Now you might already be thinking, would God really make Carrie be autistic so Ann could be a good friend to a boy who needed one? The answer is, of course He would. We as humans think in the moment, but God thinks eternally. The sixty years that I will spend taking care of Carrie are a blink of an eye to God. Would God really saddle me with an autistic child just so some six-year-old kid I'd never met would have an understanding classmate? You betcha. And as unfair as it seems on paper, I'm at peace with it.

How can I know the eternal consequences of Ann being Mitch's friend? Maybe Mitch's parents have been fighting the school system to the point that they're tired of it all, or maybe they look at their little boy and know his sadness is from being lonely, and they thank God for sending Ann to be Mitch's friend. If this one gift renews their faith and their outlook on life and renews their belief in salvation, was it worth it? Maybe not to me, but certainly to Mitch and his family, and most definitely to God.

It is thoughts like that one that keep me going. I do not know God's plan, but I know He has one. And I don't mean to sound blissfully ignorant. I would love to stand in God's presence for just a minute and DEMAND that He tell me what the point of all this hurt was. But for now, it is enough that I trust He has a point to all this. He has to.

Here is how our faith helps us be good parents to Carrie:

1. For better or worse, she is our gift from God. Just ask any of the millions of childless couples out there. I wasn't specific, I didn't tell God I wanted a perfect baby with the right color eyes or matching dimples when she smiles. Not that He would have listened if it wasn't part of His plan.

2. Know that you are being taken care of by a higher power. Yes, this is way out of your control but you can do it, with help.

3. My attitude has always been one of, "It could be so much worse," and it brings me peace in so many areas of my life. Sometimes my job sucks, but I have a job. Gas prices are way too high, but God has given me the abundance to afford a nice car and the gas to go in it. Yes, Carrie is autistic. My brother and his wife cannot have any children. It could be worse.

Chapter 23: Learning to Laugh

Already you're probably thinking to yourself, "Why is this crazy woman offering me laughing lesson?" You have put up with me all this time, kindly ignoring my pithy remarks and tolerating my very judgmental comments. I appreciate that, but more importantly, I hope your autistic child comes to appreciate it, too, because it means that you will put up with an insanely aggravating person in order to do the best you can for your child. Good job!

Maybe the single most important thing you can do for your child is laugh. At everything. At yourself, your situation, even your child. Because your child would make you laugh if he was normal, wouldn't he? Wouldn't you call your mother on the phone or annoy your co-workers with ANOTHER funny story about something hilarious your child did? Why is it suddenly irreverent to laugh just because your kid is developmentally delayed?

Don't go me wrong, obviously I'm not implying that you should laugh AT your child, but it's perfectly fine to laugh at the things he says or does. Because they're probably funny. Your child is basically an outsider in our world and how many Hollywood movies have been churned out and turned into box-office moneymakers about aliens or foreigners coming to our world and trying to fit in?

More importantly, some days the only thing that's going to keep you from driving your car through a crowded fast food restaurant and letting the authorities take you away will be your ability to laugh at life. It's going to save you.

Do you know someone who has to complain at all times, no matter what? That person who makes you cringe when you see their name on your caller ID because you know you will be trapped on the phone for two hours listening to her complain about her physical ailments? Or that woman you see in the grocery store who makes you dodge behind a giant inflatable potato chip display because you just don't have the time today to listen to her whine about her kids AGAIN? Then you're nicer than I am, because when someone like that invades my time and tries to spread her personal black cloud over my day, I respond with something like, "Wow, that must really suck. That's almost as bad as having a handicapped child."

The strange thing is, I'm really thinking to myself, "Good grief, if my life were that bad I'd have jumped off the cliff by now." My life is freaking awesome compared to some of the stories people have cornered me with. All because I'm able to wake up every day wondering what surprises are going to be waiting for me.

Trust me, I'm not just a better person than you. And no, I wish I was, but I'm not even on better pills than you. I'm not on anything stronger than Flintstone vitamins. But here's the thing: after that first initial argument with my husband over Carrie's treatment, the one where I actually had to call a divorce lawyer for an appointment, I made a command decision. That's not going to be me. I had read early on in Carrie's diagnosis that fifty percent of marriages in our country end in divorce, but that number jumps to EIGHTY PERCENT if there is a handicapped child in the family. What the hell? What in the world was going on with these kids that it was causing people to rip apart their families? My husband and I both decided right then that it was not going to happen to us.

I wish I could say it's been a cakewalk ever since making that decision. But it's not. We have our good days and our bad days just as much as any other family. I even strangely recall one argument in particular during which I said, "I won't divorce you because I won't put the girls through that, but I sure as hell don't mind making them orphans!" Oh c'mon, I'm kidding. No, I'm not.

The difference is the laughing. My husband and I are possibly two of the strangest people on the planet. The things that strike us as funny are so uncommonly bizarre that most normal people would run away screaming. My high school students are always amazed and possibly appalled that I enjoy the show SOUTH PARK. I don't enjoy it because I'm an idiot, but because some days I need an excuse to laugh and animated fourth graders using copious amounts of profanity are sometimes all I've got. Laughter is a conscious choice activity.

Here are some of the ways we're able to bring laughter into our lives:

1. Teach your kids the fine art of the stupid joke. Better yet, buy a cheap-and-cheesy joke book, the more knock knock jokes the better. You will laugh for hours. Of course, so will I, envisioning you on a ten-hour car trip to Arizona with any and all of your kids telling knock knock jokes the whole way.

2. Your day will be a whole lot funnier the moment you realize you're not Superman. As I write these very words I have seriously just informed my family that I am done playing restaurant at every meal. From now on I will cook basic ingredients and they will assemble it any way they choose. Right this very minute there is a skillet of cooked hamburger meat on the counter, along with a bowl of cooked peas, and some noodles boiling away in water. I have placed a bag of shredded cheddar cheese, some seasonings, and some salsa on the counter as well. Dinner is served. If they don't like it, the pantry contains other food stuffs and the pizza delivery place is pre-programmed into the phone. But I'm not going to go nuts trying to keep everyone's food tastes and dietary requirements in line. And I'm laughing a lot about that!

3. Make a determined effort to find happiness. I'm not trying to imply that people with special needs children no longer

have the capacity to be happy. Far from it. But some days the effort of being his parent is going to wear you down. So make the choice that you will be happy, no matter what.

Chapter 24: Technology

This chapter just kind of randomly plops itself into this book because it's something I thought of at the last minute. And also because I started this book quite some time ago and Carrie has aged up into a self-sufficiency that has come about in large part because of technology.

Carrie doesn't use any specific kinds of assistive technology, although there is a lot of it on the market. As a parent who has never had to find or buy any assistive technology for her child's needs, be careful of taking my advice here! But I do have a lot of experience with internet searches that led me to snake oil cures for my child's autism, so maybe I'm just a little more cautious than I should be.

When Carrie was in second grade, we experimented with getting her a tiny little laptop computer to use in school. Her school is awesome about special education, and they readily agreed that they would incorporate it into her work once I offered to provide it. At the time, she was doing really well academically, but was struggling to keep her behavior in check for the entire school day.

After some thought, I wondered if Carrie was actually struggling to cope in an exhausting school day. I bought the laptop hoping that making her school work just that much easier could help her behavior, and luckily, it solved most of her problems. By not having to spend so much of her day using a pencil (handwriting has always been a big area of weakness for her), Carrie was able to more easily complete her work without tantrums and needing few breaks.

This year, I happened to buy myself an iPad for work and found that Carrie really took it. Something about not having to press all the little buttons on a keyboard really appealed to her. She's a pro at swiping her little fingers across the screen.

There are a lot of important things to remember about investing in any kind of technology for your child. First, not all of it is going to be helpful for every child on the spectrum because these children are as different as any other children. Also, be wary of letting the technology be so prevalent in your child's life that he or she is crippled if it's not available.

There are some really awesome resources out there on what and how technology can be practical for your child. You will have to spend some time searching for it. You will also need a plan of action for how the technology will be used. Is your child going to use a computer all day long in class? Will you try to allow some technology, some hand written work?

Here are some things that were helpful for Carrie with technology:

1. First, talk to everyone about it. Ask your child's teachers, school counselor, support group parents, and more about what has been helpful for them. Keep a list of things that worked and didn't work, but more importantly find out what issues their children had and that were helpful.

2. Confirm it with your child's school that any devices you purchase will be allowed for school, but more importantly, find out if any technology will be more of a disruption than a help. Schools are not required to let you bring technology of your own for school use and it's important to have it clearly spelled out in your child's IEP who will be providing the technology and how it will be used during the school day.

3. On that note, there are times when schools provide the technology that a special ed student will use, but there are also limits on how much funding they have for that. Since I was the one who felt that a laptop might help Carrie, I insisted on paying for it. In return, the school promised me that they would allow Carrie to use it as much as possible since I was the one investing in it.

4. There are very good resources that can help you with your decision. My favorite is a website called Apps for Children with Special Needs, found at a4cwsn.com. This website is a one-man operation in which a dedicated father literally buys apps with his own money, makes a video of himself using it in order to show you what its capabilities are, then

posts the video online. He is on this mission in order to keep parents of special needs children from wasting a single penny on an app or device that doesn't do what their children need, especially since some of these apps can cost hundreds of dollars. The site also has a strong Facebook community.

5. Beware of the crutch issue I mentioned early in this book. Assistive technology is exactly what it sounds like, a form of assistance. It can't be the only tool your child can use.

Chapter 25: Knowing Autism

This is additional information that I'm throwing into this book because I often hear from people who have read my book. The single common thread I always hear from people who reach out to me is this: "I don't have an autistic child, but my

_____ has autism." Sometimes it's their nephew or their neighbor, sometimes it's their child's classmate. But ask around and you'll realize that everyone knows someone with autism.

I'm thrilled that so many people have read this book because they want to be a better person in the life of someone affected in some way by autism. I actually did a Google search one day that led me to find out that this book has been illegally downloaded over a thousand times on one ebook piracy site alone, and sure, that's several hundred dollars stolen from my family. But I can't get mad because it's also over a thousand people who are trying to know and love someone with autism and those people, misguided though they may be, are now better equipped to help a child. On a side note, many of those illegal downloads are in countries where any kind of handicap is considered a taboo or seen as a curse, so hopefully the book is working to exact change on a larger scale.

So what do you do when your hands are tied? How do even begin to help? The first answer is you already did. Just because you even wanted to understand the child or what the family is going through means you are already one more team member on their sides.

Here are ways you can really know someone with autism:

1. Talk. Don't stop calling the parents, don't skip playdates. Don't avoid the issue. Trust me, I know Carrie's autistic, even if you don't feel comfortable saying anything about it. You're not going to hurt my feelings by acknowleding the truth. Be willing to ask questions about what you don't undestand so you can be better equipped to be a source of support.

2. My sister-in-law just started a special needs baseball program because of Carrie. Her two sons are huge into the city league sports programs and so my sister-in-law planned this whole low-pressure, low attendance program built with the needs of kids like Carrie in mind. She got enough sponsors to pay for all the equipment and uniforms because she has seen the cruel amounts of money we have had to pay for Carrie's care. Provide opportunities for children to be included while realizing that including them doesn't mean the same thing for every family/

3. Offer your time and your help, even if it's in bizarre ways. Carrie wanted to have a sleepover just like her big sister

does, but she doesn't like to see people she knows when they aren't where they "belong." So I invited my friend to spend the night and bring her daughter. My friend is an awesome person who would do anything for Carrie, including pack up a bag and go to a slumber party at age 35.

4. Some of the best friends I have are the ones who just acknowledge that Carrie is different and they make allowances. Meals are planned around crazy things in Carrie's schedule, like after giving her some time to play on a computer. If she gets restless in a movie theater, they take her to go look at the coming attractions posters instead of rolling their eyes and sighing. I'm not asking for outrageous whims, but they know that I am Carrie's mother every single day, the least they can do is take the load off me once in a while.

Conclusion

I attended an autism education conference once and one speaker in particular made a profound proclamation: "Autism is not a death sentence, but it is a life sentence."

When he said that, I shattered just a little bit. Up until that point, it had never really occurred to me that Carrie was never going to leave home, that I would never retire to my little cottage in the woods, venturing out to spend time with my grandchildren or to travel. My dreams of spending my golden years bouncing around America in my rusty old RV fizzled like a leaky balloon. Instead, I was going to be the eighty-five-year-old woman dragging her fifty-five year old daughter through Walmart once a week to buy our groceries. Hopefully we wouldn't be eating cat food.

So I don't let myself think about tomorrow, or next year, or when I'm eighty-five. If I do, I'll miss out on the amazing things that are happening today. Today my daughter told me she loves me. Today she tried to pick out her own clothes. Today she came home and told me something she did at school without me having to play Twenty Questions. It's not huge, but for today, it's enough.

I have always imagined the metaphor of Carrie's life being similar to her hanging from a cliff. It feels as though I'm holding her hand as she dangles above certain death and the only thing that will keep her from falling is my ability to hang on. If I'm too weak and I let go, she's gone. And she's not able to do her part to help me. She's looking at my struggling face and smiling, but the whole time I'm screaming at her to hold on, to climb up, to try to reach the branch above her. And she won't, because she doesn't know how. It's up to me to save her.

That's a very unfair, unrealistic expectation for myself. But I'm her mom and I'm going to do all I can. I am strong enough to hold on to her for as long as it takes. She will not slip out of my hands, and the harder she tries to fall because it's the easy thing to do, the more I'm going to dig my nails in and hold on to her. That's all I can ask of myself. And you can do the same for your child.

Printed in Great Britain
by Amazon.co.uk, Ltd.,
Marston Gate.

3259889R00074